SYMPOSIUM

The Intellectual in Politics

THE INTELLECTUAL IN POLITICS

GUNNAR HECKSCHER

DANIEL COSIO VILLEGAS

FRANCISCO MIRÓ QUESADA

SIR DENIS BROGAN

MERLE FAINSOD

KLAUS MEHNERT

JOHN BRADEMAS

EUGENE J. MCCARTHY

EDITED WITH AN INTRODUCTION BY DR. H. MALCOLM MACDONALD

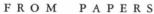

FROM PAPERS DELIVERED IN APRIL 1965

THE UNIVERSITY OF TEXAS, AUSTIN, TEXAS

published by

THE HUMANITIES RESEARCH CENTER

THE UNIVERSITY OF TEXAS

Distributed by

UNIVERSITY OF TEXAS PRESS

AUSTIN, TEXAS 78712

Printed in the U.S.A. by the University of Texas Printing Division

Reprint from THE TEXAS QUARTERLY

CONTENTS : THE INTELLECTUAL IN POLITICS

BIOGRAPHICAL NOTES

H. MALCOLM MACDONALD is Professor of Government and Chairman of the Department of Government at The University of Texas. His fields of interest are political theory and jurisprudence.

DR. GUNNAR HECKSCHER, Professor of Political Science at the University of Stockholm and Parliamentary Leader of the Swedish Conservative Party. He is one of the outstanding intellectuals on the contemporary Swedish scene.

DR. DANIEL COSIO VILLEGAS, until 1963 president of El Colegio de Mexico, which he founded—Mexico's leading research institute.

Founder of Fondo de Cultura Economica—Mexico's leading publishing house for cultural and economic works.

Initiator, editor, director, and collaborator of the multi-volumed Historia Moderna de Mexico.

Mexico's permanent delegate for several years to the United Nations Economic and Social Council and president of that organization in 1959.

AMBASSADOR FRANCISCO MIRÓ QUESADA, Professor of Philosophy and Ideologist in the Accion Popular Party of President Fernando Belaunde Terry.

Served until recently in the Belaunde administration as Minister of Education.

Currently, Ambassador of Peru to the United Nations.

SIR DENIS BROGAN, Professor of Political Science and Philosophy at Peterhouse, Cambridge University, England. Widely travelled in the United States, which he has visited on numerous occasions, and known for his works on American and British political subjects.

PROFESSOR MERLE FAINSOD, Professor of Government and Director of the Harvard University Library. One of America's leading authorities on Soviet Russia.

DR. KLAUS MEHNERT, Professor of Political Science at the Institute of Technology, Aachen (Aix-la-Chapelle) and editor of Osteuropa; author of Asien, Moskau and wir (1956), Der Sowjetmensch (1958), Peking and Moskau (1962).

REPRESENTATIVE JOHN BRADEMAS, Member of the House of Representatives from Indiana, a former Rhodes Scholar, Phi Beta Kappa, and Professor of Political Science. He has represented the State of Indiana in the United States Congress since 1959.

SENATOR EUGENE J. MCCARTHY, Member of the United States Senate from Minnesota since 1958, and author of numerous works on American Government, including *A Liberal Answer to the Conservative Challenge*, 1964.

HE FOLLOWING PAPERS WERE PREPARED FOR DELIVERY AT A CONFERENCE, "The Intellectual in Politics," held at the University of Texas in April of 1965.[1] The theme of the conference was spawned from a conversation with Daniel Cosio Villegas on tre divergent roles played by American and Mexican intellectuals in the politics of their respective countries. The idea seemed worthy of fuller investigation and broadened into the present inquiry on the role of the intellectual in politics in the western world. Señod Cosio agreed to contribute a paper on Mexico and was joined by a distinguished group of scholars who undertook to comment on the problem as it manifested itself in Peru, Germany, Sweden, Great Britain, the USSR, and the United States.

The similarities and divergencies of the views of the participants will be apparent to the reader and will not be recapitulated here. Suffice it to say that there emerged from the conference a consensus on the necessity of the intellectual, however defined, to remain true to his task of being what Julien Benda has called "the conscience of humanity."

Plato initially defined the role of the intellectual in society and hence in politics. For him, our term "intellectual" would equate with "philosopher, the lover of wisdom." For Plato, the philosopher is an individual whose inner dæmon drives him to seek truth through the disciplined use of reason, an arduous enterprise which few are capable of sustaining. Those who persevere, however, are assured of penetrating to an apprehension of the nature of things, to an understanding of cosmic reality, on the basis of which they can structure balanced and harmonious lives. Philosophical knowledge, accordingly, is the intellectual appreciation of that which in itself is most real; unaffected by time, place, or the thinker's comprehension of it. It thus differs from the "opinions" of the Sophists, or the "illusions" of the masses, which deal only with the appearances of things.

That such a view might well lead to the intellectual's withdrawal from society and his retirement into a hermit's life of contemplation was obvious to Plato. Hence he charges the philosopher, if he is to perform his function well, with the obligation of placing his insights at the service of mankind. This is the lesson of the allegory of the cave in which the inquiring mind, emancipated from the darkness of opinion

[1] The holding of this conference was made possible by a grant from the University's Excellence Fund. The conference was sponsored by the Department of Government and arranged by a committee composed of Professors H. M. Macdonald, Karl Schmitt, James Steintrager, W. D. Webb, and B. F. Wright. Chancellor H. H. Ransom and Dean Alton Burdine contributed valuable encouragement and support. Technical assistance and cooperation were provided by Mrs. Frances Hudspeth of the Humanities Research Center and Mrs. Mary Hirth of the Academic Center. Editorial advice was given by Mrs. Margaret McGrade. To all these persons the Committee expresses its thanks and appreciation.

and conjecture, experiences the illuminating light of truth, only to be told that it must not bask content in its rays but return to the cave and interpret the nature of reality to the inhabitants. Thus, two essential characteristics of the intellectual which combine to form his historic mission emerge: a passion for truth and the duty to transmit that truth, so far as he comprehends it, to his fellows.

But danger lurks here, too, for to perform his function properly, Plato's intellectual must be a true philosopher king, that is, one who really knows truth and who applies his knowledge objectively, unswayed by egotism, pride, or self-interest. If he falls short in these respects, he is in danger of becoming a fanatic or a crank, succumbing to the sin of *hybris,* and ceasing to be a philosopher at all. That such perverted individuals have appeared in history, with unpleasant results for mankind, is admitted; that this must be the fate of all intellectuals is denied.

Aristotle showed a way out of this dilemma. Pledged as firmly as Plato to the proposition of the intellectual's commitment to truth, he tempered its application by affirming the essential contingency of human existence. The intellectual was reminded that no individual can know truth in its fullness, and that so far as he comes to know it in part, his ability to communicate and effectuate it in practice is conditioned by the specific situation in which he finds himself. The intellectual must still return to the cave, but in so doing he must submit to its environment, patiently work to change it and to induce its denizens to realize their potentials; but he must always be conscious that his efforts will be only partially successful.

It is against this limitation, the limitation of the possible, that many intellectuals have rebelled, be they the ideologues of the eighteenth century or the social engineers of the twentieth. Convinced of their own assumed omnipotence as "philosopher kings," and of the worth of their respective utopias, they have sought so to structure men as to achieve perfection here and now, and in striving for heaven often established hell. Others, more mindful of Aristotle and hence conscious of contingency, while not abandoning their vision of what might be, have sought to realize it in terms of the limitations imposed by the nature of man and society.

The need to recognize contingency underlies Señor Cosio's analysis of the role of the intellectual in Mexico. There the social structure is such that the intellectual is prevented from directly influencing political decisions, a possibility, incidentally, envisioned by Plato in the *Republic,* in which he notes that such a situation results not from the incompetency of the intellectuals to contribute significantly to the solution of problems but from the refusal of society to attend to their advice. Under such circumstances, intellectuals are compelled to operate in subtle and limited ways, indirectly and by personal example, as best they can. This is unhealthy for both the intellectuals and society and often results in the building up of frustration within the intellectual class which then finds an outlet either in the espousal of impractical, utopian idealism, as was the case with the Narodnik movement in Tsarist Russia, or in an attempt to cut the Gordian knot by violent revolutionary action, as in the case of Lenin, Trotsky, and the Bolshevik movement. In such cases, the intellectual betrays

H. MALCOLM MACDONALD

his calling either by ending as an ineffectual, though often heroic, dreamer or as a fanatic who sacrifices virtue to power.

Whatever the intellectual's contribution to the fermentation of a revolutionary situation may be, his ability to influence events after a victorious revolution is usually marginal. Once the consolidation of the new regime begins, he is displaced by the nonintellectual organizational man, adept at the manipulation of power. Witness the victory of Stalin over both Trotsky and Bukharin.

It is for these and other reasons that some have questioned the desirability of the intellectual's actively participating in politics, preferring that he remain detached from the conflict, concerning himself more with advice and criticism than with deeds. Klaus Mehnert, in his paper, adopts this view and argues that the intellectual should not enter politics, since he lacks a sense of political timing, an ability to reach decisions, and consequently cannot operate efficiently in the political arena. Hans Morgenthau has expressed similar reservations, contending that by accepting government office the intellectual abrogates his objectivity, loses his freedom of action, and hence abandons his true function of passing impartial judgments on events. If this be true, then those who participate in "presidential brain trusts" cease to be intellectuals in the correct meaning of the word. By implication also, those intellectuals who engaged in the Viet Nam "teach-ins" were truer to their calling than if they had elected to serve as advisors to the State Department. Hans Morgenthau, it is interesting to note, has played both roles.

During debates concerning the U.S. policy in Viet Nam, those intellectuals who, like McGeorge Bundy, appeared as spokesmen for the Administration and defenders of the official policy, were denounced by some as renegades from the intellectual camp, members of the "establishment" and dangerously akin to those Sophists whom Plato accused of being willing to advocate any cause for a fee. The "establishment," on its side, countered by accusing the instigators of the "teach-ins" of being ignorant of the facts and disdainful of practicalities, and ended by enjoining them to refrain from criticism until further study of reality would enlighten them to the correctness of the government's policy. Regardless of the merits of these respective positions, the controversy underlines the dilemma that confronts the intellectual when he attempts to participate actively in policy formation.

Prescinding from the problem of the effectiveness of the intellectuals as practicing politicians, one has no doubt of their ability, under favorable circumstances, to influence significantly the climate of political opinion. This is especially true in societies in which the communication media are well developed, the dissemination of information uncensored, and the population literate. In the United States, where public education has become a fetish and the channels of communication are open, the intellectuals have exercised considerable influence. Pundits like Walter Lippmann, commentators like Edward Morgan, and the contributors to the numerous journals of opinion have found large audiences which consciously or unconsciously base their opinions on what they read in their newspapers or see and hear on their television and radio sets. By any definition, not all of these practitioners of the communication arts are intellectuals, but many of them are, and their influence is extensive. It is among the intellectuals engaged in education, however, that one finds the major force working to mold long-term opinion in America.

That the views of those engaged in teaching university and college students and in preparing the teachers who will instruct in the secondary and grade schools have had a pervasive effect upon American society necessitates no elaborate proof. The alteration of traditional moral attitudes in America since World War I, the rise, growth, and general acceptance of the social service state, the swing from isolationism to internationalism have in considerable measure resulted from the promulgation of new ideas and approaches by members of the academic community.

Their task has been to interpret to their fellow citizens and to the youth of the nation the new requirements of an increasingly complex and technical society and, in so doing, of necessity to posit the values by which this brave new world can be legitimized. Whether they have done their task well or ill is not our concern here; that they have undertaken it with discernible results is evident.

If this is conceded, then the responsibility of the intellectual engaged in the educational enterprise is indeed an awesome one. He must guard against substituting subjective opinions and prejudices in the place of knowledge and truth and be constantly mindful of his obligation to be objective, yet not so objective as to be unwilling to be definite. He must have vision and reasoned goals for which he strives, while safeguarding himself against the futilities of impractical idealism by his remembrance of the limitations imposed by contingency. He will, if he is honest, be keenly conscious of his responsibility for what he says, since what he teaches even casually will be believed and followed by many of his hearers with consequences which he cannot foresee.

It is submitted, then, that the American intellectuals, especially those engaged in education, have contributed more significantly to the rationale of the "American Way of Life" than they or the public have realized, and that they have done so primarily by challenging modes of thought which have become obsolete and thus, as the Marxists would put it, "fetters upon progress." This is all to the good provided that it is borne in mind that while contingent solutions are always temporary and must yield to the dynamic of change, there still remain underlying values which do not change but which do require constant reinterpretation to meet new challenges.

This realization creates a crisis amongst intellectuals. The Young Turks of yesterday, whose solutions are now becoming ossified, are challenged, even as they themselves had challenged their predecessors, by a still younger generation of thinkers.

In intellectual circles there is an increasing repudiation of the formulas of optimistic liberal utilitarianism, which are viewed as having fulfilled their creative purposes, and now need to be replaced by more persuasive premises if a humane social order is to be achieved. These stresses and strains are healthy, manifesting an

H. MALCOLM MACDONALD

awareness and acceptance of responsibility on the part of the intellectuals. They underscore the intellectual's refusal to accept the freezing of contingent, although originally meaningful, constructs into infallible dogmas.

The freedom and openness of American society permit these developments and encourage the reinterpretation of truth in response to new requirements. On the other hand, in the Soviet Union, where the intellectualism of Marxism has hardened into a dogmatic orthodoxy and the accommodation of practice to theory can be accomplished only by an esoteric and complex process of rationalization, the continued unfolding of truth has become difficult if not impossible. Although the USSR has both modern communication facilities and a rising rate of literacy, its intellectuals have been thwarted by a rigid censorship imposed in defense of dogma. Yet even a half century of Communist indoctrination has not been able to suppress the intellectuals, nor destroy the desire of individuals to know and speak the truth. With each thaw, with each momentary relaxation of control, the intellectuals, like the phoenix of old, have risen up to testify to man's indomitable will to be himself. Merle Fainsod's paper illustrates this point with grace and sensitivity. Although the intellectuals with whom he deals are artists, writers, and poets, they too are political, for they cry out against the system, bureaucracy, and selfish power, against privilege unearned, and for the right of men to be free.

Thus it seems that the intellectual is one of the constants, and hence necessities, of history. He appears as a gadfly in every age and his contribution to politics in diverse forms is impressive, although it has often been manipulated by politicians in manners not consistent with his aims. His greatest temptation has been to succumb to arrogance and cynicism; his saving grace has been humility and patience. The basis of his strength lies in his capacity to come to terms with himself and, by introspection, to reason through to an understanding of his nature and destiny. Only when he understands himself and has grasped truth as he conceives it, can he turn, confidently and effectively, to the task of influencing his environment. Ultimately, then, a return to the cave is inescapable for the genuine intellectual; how he then comports himself will depend in part upon his own talents and abilities and in part upon the situation with which he is confronted and on which he must act. With this in mind, we turn to the following essays in which the intellectual is discussed both as an individual and in relation to specific situations in which he has appeared.

GUNNAR HECKSCHER : *The Role of the Intellectual in Politics—*
A Swedish View

THE PROBLEM CONFRONTING US IN THIS CONFERENCE IS ONE OF POLITICAL
sociology. In contrast to most other sociological problems, however, it can
hardly be approached by quantitative methods except to a small extent. The
important thing is less the exact number of intellectuals in clearly political functions

at different periods of our history than their actual influence on political decisions. Moreover, it is a problem that makes it difficult to avoid bias, or at least not to allow one's reasoning to be colored by one's own environment, experience and opinions. Further, in dealing with the problem we shall find that the choice of conclusions is, to a great extent, a question of the approach. There will be comments by other speakers and writers, no doubt from different approaches. Perhaps I should state at the outset that I am writing *both* as a political scientist *and* as an active politician.

Obviously, with any approach to the problem generalizations are required. I shall attempt to present some sort of framework: some fundamental generalizations, chiefly with regard to definitions as well as to backgrounds; secondly, a few of what I regard as the more important general problems; and, finally, some comments of a more subjective nature.

Whom are we talking about? That is to say, what categories do we regard as intellectuals? Are we going to use a wide definition or a narrower one? In approaching this question, it may be useful to remind ourselves of certain groups of "intellectuals" who have empirically proved to be important to political life.

In the Middle Ages, the question was easily answered. Intellectuals were found almost exclusively in the ranks of the clergy. Political influence was wielded not only by the Church as such but also by its leading men in secular capacities. There is a document from my country which I have always found illuminating. Dating from the fifteenth century and embodying a decision of the Council of the Realm, it leaves certain functions in the hands of "those of the Council who are able to read." Admittedly, Sweden in those days was rather backward, but a couple of hundred years earlier the situation had been much the same all over. The definition would include mainly a number of bishops and abbots—in fact, it was because only the Church provided real intellectual training that its representatives could exercise so much political influence and that the type of politician represented today by Archbishop Makarios was so prevalent and so important in medieval times.

In modern times, the influence of the Church remains important in many countries. On the other hand, Archbishop Makarios stands almost unique in his double capacity of political and religious leader. Our interest, therefore, must be concentrated on other groups.

Let us begin with the fact that practicing *lawyers* dominate, or used to dominate, political life in a great number of Western countries. I believe this is still true of the United States and that until very recently it was also true in France. In Great Britain, legal training was more usual than any other form of professional training for members of Parliament, and I believe the same to be true of most of the other countries in the British Commonwealth.

At one time, the medical profession was widely represented in French politics. This was an exception to other countries, but it has to be admitted that *doctors* have a certain way about them, a particular capacity for inspiring public confidence.

Another profession which, at times and in certain places, has enjoyed great poli-

GUNNAR HECKSCHER

tical importance is that of *military officers.* The officer will always be a good political candidate, not only in revolutionary countries but, as well, in others having recent experience of war. Quite frequently, the armed forces as such exercise considerable political power; we have but to think of France before General de Gaulle's rise to power. In most countries it is obvious that the military profession is an intellectual one and that its political influence is based not only on glamor but also on the fact that its members are apt to think in strategical terms. This, of course, is much the same as thinking in political terms.

Again at certain times and in certain places, the body of opinion of *university students* has been politically important. This is true in many countries today. As a Swede, I particularly recall the role played by university students in the "Scandinavist" movement in the nineteenth century—an important, albeit in the end an abortive, movement.

Journalists, it is interesting to note, have, in most countries, been active chiefly through their newspapers and not by crossing, in their own right, the threshold of parliamentary life. Here, however, Sweden is an exception, for its Parliament has always contained a considerable group of active journalists, and a number of Swedish political leaders have had, to a greater or lesser degree, journalistic experience. This has been especially true of the parties to the left of center.

A specific intellectual group is that of *civil servants.* Positions in the civil service are, in most countries, incompatible with parliamentary functions—a principle derived from the United Kingdom, where it was introduced to eliminate the corruptive practices of the eighteenth century. Some countries, however, present exceptions. In Sweden, as in Finland, in Norway, as in Denmark, it is still possible to sit in Parliament while holding administrative office. Although the practice is becoming rare, it is still not unheard of. On the other hand, civil servants are politically very important, even where they are debarred from parliamentary functions. It may, in fact, be asked whether they do not exercise even more influence outside Parliament than they could ever wield inside it. Few ministers are sufficiently well versed in the details of their administrative work to avoid being influenced by definite views held by their own civil servants.

Finally, we are of course thinking of *university professors.* Small though this group may be, its position is interesting as an illustration of our general problem. As early as 1848, the first abortive attempt at an all-German Parliament earned the nickname of *"Das Professorenparlament."* Today it is enough to mention the names of Ludwig Erhard and Carlo Schmid to make it clear that political leadership in free Germany still lies largely in the hands of academic persons. To a lesser extent this has been true of Sweden, as well as of Finland, where K. J. Stahlberg rose to be President of the Republic and Ragnar Furuhjelm was for a long time the leader of the Swedish-speaking minority. In the United Kingdom, the role of "dons" of all categories has been increasing in the postwar period. Even in the United States,

Woodrow Wilson was President for two terms, and Paul Douglas, presently an influential senator, has been mentioned as a Presidential candidate.

Thus, it is obvious that many with an academic or otherwise intellectual training exercise great political influence practically everywhere. On the basis of this observation, we may attempt a definition of the intellectual.

For my own part, I would include under this term all those who by their professional training and/or experience have developed the habit of studying politics as such, or one or more of the important parts of the subject matter dealt with in politics. This means that we include those who have benefited from a formal intellectual education, whether or not they have acquired a particularly intelligent understanding of political problems. Conversely, the definition excludes a great number of people who may have such intelligent understanding but who have acquired it entirely by practical experience in politics as such, without being specifically trained for the purpose. The definition is useful on the supposition that the kind of professional training or experience referred to should aim at developing the habit of critical analysis to be used in approaching definite types of problems that confront those who wield power in modern societies.

Having attempted this definition, we may next deal with another and equally important aspect of our problem: the variations in the role of intellectuals appearing in different types of societies.

The most obvious distinction is that between developed and underdeveloped countries. Obviously, the role of intellectuals is greatly influenced by the extent to which their capacities are widely spread among *non*intellectuals. To express it more concretely: where "the man in the street (or in the village) can at least roughly cope with the intellectual aspects of political problems, where he is able to read not only newspapers but even books, he stands far less in need of assistance from the intellectual than he otherwise might. But we must not be blind to the fact that there are peoples in the world whose conditions in this respect are not unlike those of the people of medieval Europe. Thus, where the level of general education is low, the role of the professionally intellectual population grows in proportion to the complications faced by such a society.

In highly developed Western societies, those who are "intelligent without being intellectuals," *e.g.* farmers, union leaders, and others, compete successfully in the political field. Their attitudes are often colored by a profound distrust of their professionally intellectual brethren. In underdeveloped societies, those who are "intellectuals without being intelligent" are able to exercise an influence out of all proportion to their capacities.

But the difference is not solely one of underdeveloped and developed societies. There is also the difference between emerging independent states and countries having a more stable political tradition. It is by no means certain that emerging states are based upon underdeveloped societies. The examples of Poland, Czechoslovakia, Finland, and the Baltic states in the period between the World Wars prove that

GUNNAR HECKSCHER

even where the new state is based upon a fairly well-developed social structure, the very fact of its being a new political entity leads to greater reliance on intellectuals to fill the many leading positions which have suddenly become available.

If we limit our study to countries with a stable constitutional structure, based upon a well-developed society, we still find considerable variation. This is largely a matter of national tradition. The role of the clergy in European countries a few hundred years ago may be recalled. To become a clergyman—"a clerk"—was the common man's road to recognized social position. Again, the example of Archbishop Makarios can be cited to illustrate a situation otherwise fairly unusual in Europe today. But even if this is now so, the historic role of the "clerks" created a traditional respect for the intellectual and a habit of confiding several important functions to him. No European country has cut loose from this tradition; it is perhaps strongest in Germany.

At the other extreme, we are apt to think of the United States. The American public traditionally takes a dim view of "eggheads." This was true in pioneer times, but it is nonetheless true today. Some may remember the case of Charles Merriam, the professor of political science who tried to become mayor of Chicago. His opponent was a man of the lowest quality who won the election because he always referred to Merriam as "the Prof"; the electorate of Chicago apparently preferred to vote for just anybody, provided he was not a professor. Even in the United States, however, this is not always true, as evidenced by the very different experience of Woodrow Wilson.

It is perhaps likely that this American attitude is undergoing some modification today. On the other hand, it is also probably beginning at the same time to find a place in a considerable sector of European opinion. Nevertheless, the positions on the two sides of the Atlantic Ocean are very different. In Germany, "Herr Professor" is still an honored title and not—as it was in Chicago—a bad name in politics, and every other German politician is what would be, in the United States, called an egghead. We may also cite the examples to be found in the United Kingdom, where what our British friends call "the Establishment" consists largely of what Americans would term "intellectuals," although with the further proviso that the persons in question should have acquired their training at the "right" schools and universities.

Assuming, then, that intellectuals do play a part in political life in practically all sorts of societies, we come to the next question: what, in fact, is their function, and what should it properly be? Should they play the part of political leaders, should they be visionaries, pointing to a road that is far ahead of the one to be followed in the near future—or should they appear chiefly as experts, putting their knowledge at the disposal of those actively engaged in decision making?

It is, I suppose, more or less agreed that politics is a question of power and that the function of political science is to study different methods of exercising power. But there is another question, namely: *for which purpose is political power sought?*

It is a popular assumption that the main objective of politicians is personal aggrandizement. To a varying extent, this may be true, as it unquestionably was in the eighteenth century in Britain. Another objective of recognized importance is that of group interest: organized or amorphous group attempt, through their representatives or by means of discreet blackmail, to compel political authorities to do their bidding, presumably in the economic or other interests of their members. Finally, we have Edmund Burke's definition of a party, which by implication involves also a certain approach to politics: a body of men who have united to further the public interest in accordance with principles upon which they are agreed. To a greater or lesser extent, all these aspects enter the picture, but opinions vary considerably as to their relative importance. For reasons that are equally obvious, opinions on the role of intellectuals will vary accordingly.

To an increasing extent, modern society makes it necessary to use *experts* to provide the basic information essential to political decisions, as well as, in many cases, to execute these decisions. The specialized knowledge of these experts is applied, for instance, whenever civil servants provide background material for their political masters. On the other hand, it is becoming increasingly clear that politicians must also have a considerable amount of independent knowledge if they are not to become merely the tools of their own civil servants. The role of intellectuals increased in wartime in most countries; in one form or another, they were found to be exercising tremendous power, often very successfully. It can be said that the "brain trusts" of Franklin D. Roosevelt and John F. Kennedy were, in a sense, attempts to adapt these wartime practices to peace conditions. Whether or not they were successful in this respect is a question on which opinion is likely to vary widely. We must, however, remember that specialized knowledge can also be acquired by people who have had no formal intellectual training. Such genuinely manual workers as Ernest Bevin, in Great Britain, have become successful, very independent, and very knowledgeable Cabinet ministers. Another interesting fact is that the labor unions in Europe are almost invariably led by persons who have themselves risen from the ranks of the labor movement and who have had little or no formal education. Very often, leaders of this type are able, after a time, to acquire just as much knowledge and insight as their experts and to relegate the latter to more or less secondary functions.

The *ideologists,* of course, have, almost without exception, been intellectuals. Several failed to exercise direct power in their lifetimes, but in the long run they became far more powerful and important than contemporaries who held recognized official positions. Edmund Burke and Karl Marx are examples of this type of intellectual, although they are by no means the only ones. On the other side, we may cite Lenin and Masaryk, who combined the two roles of ideologist and great political leader. It may be dangerous to speak of contemporaries in this respect, but examples of both types could presumably be found in the 1960s.

The difficulty of distinguishing between the different sorts of intellectuals is per-

GUNNAR HECKSCHER

haps best clarified by a couple of illustrations. On the one hand, we have persons such as Dean Acheson, who set out as pure experts but in the end aspire to statesmanship. On the other hand, we have the problem of the attitude of university students and their organizations who sometimes find it difficult to decide whether to limit their activities to their own training and related "student problems" or to take an active part, as such, in political conflicts and developments. The problem arises notably in the new countries, but it is far from unknown elsewhere. For instance, many students and student organizations participate actively in the attempts to solve racial problems in the United States. This is obviously for ideological reasons. The immediate cause is a feeling of responsibility, ideological conviction as well as expert knowledge generate the wish to influence actual social development regardless of personal consequences.

In attempting to sort out these rather disjointed facts, the only possible conclusion seems to be that the role of intellectuals depends largely upon which attitude to politics is prevalent and can be regarded as acceptable. Is politics mainly a question of "who gets what when and how" or do we acquire wider vistas? If the role of ideologies in political parties, and consequently in politics as a whole, is still accepted as being very considerable, then there is greater need for the intellectuals at policymaking levels. If, on the contrary, we assume a very considerable amount of agreement on basic ideological standpoints and regard political questions as mainly problems of technique, then the intellectual is required chiefly as an expert and perhaps, also, to think, in a harmless fashion, about the ideologies of the past and of the distant future. For my own part, I refuse to accept the latter assumption. I do not believe that ideological conflicts are things of the past, nor do I agree to reduce the requirements for intellectual honesty in politics. And I think that it is only at a policymaking level that the intellectual can, for instance, insist on the need to observe, as a basis of society, such time-honored maxims as that of *pacta sunt servanda,* which are otherwise but too easily forgotten.

But whether or not the intellectuals play their parts successfully, they are confronted by a number of problems largely different from those appearing to other actors on the political scene. Whether or not he is intelligent, the intellectual can hardly avoid being relatively sophisticated—and sophistication undoubtedly carries its own dangers.

The system of government in Western countries is one of representative democracy, and we are apt to regard this as, on the whole, the best political system so far devised. But the intellectual is, as a person, usually not representative. The fundamental difference between his outlook and that of his electors may be hidden, but it can practically never be obviated. Suddenly, he may find himself out of tune with his own public.

To make this problem worse, there is in many contemporary societies a tendency toward what might be called egalitarian anti-intellectualism. The habit of thinking is in fact regarded by many as nearly immoral. Is it not true that the honest citizen requires nothing more than his instinct in order to distinguish between right and wrong? And is not he who insists upon analysis and nice distinctions thereby proving that there is something wrong with his instinct and with his honesty, as well?

We have stated that the capacity for critical analysis is a characteristic of the intellectual. While this may be a very useful thing, it may also generate scorn of the realities of political life. Occasionally it happens that the critical attitude of the intellectual makes him unwilling to think in terms of decision making and thus to become irresponsible. This attitude is usual, and probably also least dangerous, among such intellectuals as limit their political activities to participation in the political debates of the press and other media of communication.

The habit of analyzing problems carries other difficulties, as well. The intellectual is frequently suspected of belonging to what is sometimes called the "Kerensky type": someone who goes on deliberating on the pros and cons until the opportunities for decisive action have been lost. There is undoubtedly sometimes a considerable element of truth in this accusation, and it leads to contempt of intellectuals in political life, where decisions always have to be taken and must often be taken very quickly.

Connected with these problems is another. It is frequently stated that in politics it is not enough to be right—one must also be right at the right time. One hazard encountered by the intellectual in this respect is that of being right "too early." Because they have the habit of analysis, because they take the long-range view, intellectuals' ideas are sometimes too far ahead of those of their contemporaries and may, therefore, appear quite unrealistic.

It is obvious that politics has an attraction—often a strong attraction—for the intellectual. But what price is he willing to pay to satisfy his desire? This is largely a moral problem. Simplification is invariably required in politics. How far can the intellectual be expected to go on the road to vulgarity? He may be led to go too far— or he may not go far enough. It is not easy to strike the necessary mean between morally unwarranted oversimplification, on the one hand, and too great insistence upon specific distinctions, on the other.

Thus, the intellectual is over and over again accused of being "too clever." Julian Benda, in his book *La trahison des clercs,* refers chiefly to intellectuals in capacities other than those of actual participation in politics. It can hardly be denied, however, that there is considerable truth in his reflection that intellectuals have failed in the inter-war period, and are failing today, far too often, to fulfill what should be required of them in respect of the courage of their convictions and their willingness to resist the powers that be. That he may not appear too much of an "egghead," the intellectual sometimes becomes so cynical that his contribution to political decisions, whether given in the capacity of an expert or as an active politician, becomes next to useless.

There are, of course, other flaws in the character of the intellectual when he is seen as a political animal. Some politicians never seem to get beyond the stage of the "class president" of an American college. Others are so wrapped up in the ideas of their

GUNNAR HECKSCHER

youth that they fail to see that these theories refer to a society entirely different from the contemporary one and have, in fact, been replaced long since by new analyses and theories. Some of them are afflicted with the old-time professor's intolerant omniscience, while others are too prone to retire into a protective shell of irony. It should be noted, however, that these particular negative characteristics, while frequently irritating, have so far usually not been sufficiently serious to prevent the intellectuals in question from achieving very considerable success.

Like a typical intellectual in politics, I must end with a question mark. There is no final answer to the problem of what is the proper role of the intellectual in politics; or, if there is an answer, we do not have the means of finding out what it is. What should be required for our purpose ought actually to be a whole series of penetrating case studies from different countries and different types of society, referring to individuals with different personal characteristics. Or we might do even better with a series of really good political novels. Perhaps Allen Drury should have been included in our panel!

F EW ARE THE QUESTIONS THAT HAVE BROUGHT ABOUT SO MUCH MISUNDER-
standing as those involving the relation an intellectual might—and even should
—have with politics of his own country or of the whole world. It might be assumed that a rather appreciable portion of the disagreement derives from the fact

that the terms of the relationship, "intellectuals" and "politics," aside from being vague in themselves seem to bear a meaning that varies when controversy over them becomes animated. But that is certainly not the only origin of discord: it seems perfectly conceivable that an opinion which is valid for a certain place and time ceases to be so when one or both circumstances change. It is just as conceivable to assume that no assertion—not even the most discerning and fitting one—will suit all intellectuals of any country or of all eras. Some, it may be assumed, will be indifferent to all questions unrelated to their intellectual vein, while a *pur sang* politician may be mortally affected by a mere teaspoonful of intellectuality. Matters become more complicated if one considers more than the problem's purely theoretical point of view, the actual possibility of an intellectual's diving into politics at a given moment: it may happen that he does this with such a complete sacrifice of his intellectual talents that the dive will become fatal.

The Spanish dictionary—splendid for the definition of words that time leaves untouched—gives the following definition of the term "intellectual": "A person preferably devoted to culture of sciences and arts." This definition, in its obvious form, will be accepted without further bargaining by the habitual user of the dictionary, but it is objectionable precisely because it does not commit itself in any way. First, it is rather preposterous to assume that nowadays an individual may cultivate —*and* moreover *prefer*—"sciences" (note the plural form), and it is sheer fancy to imagine it is appropriate so to extend that culture as to include "the arts." For the time being, then, it seems necessary to use the singular form and to substitute the copulative for the disjunctive form, saying: a person preferably devoted to the culture of a science or an art.

But the greatest flaw lies in that "preference": in relation to what does it exist, or how should it be measured? Does measurement result from considering the inclination, ability, habit, or time alone? The temporary opinion would become more convenient to the innumerable Mexicans who write or claim to write, when actually what they "prefer" is to spend their lives near a telephone that may bring an offer of a cabinet post or at least that of a department head. Under such circumstances, they write (if they ever write) not for the *sake* of writing, but just to call attention to their political assets. By so acting, they think they effect politics, even though they actually do not, for politics is active by definition.

For all this, an English dictionary that refers to an intellectual as a person "endowed with a good intellect and culture" seems closer to the truth; it would be one who, besides being cultured and learned, has, and *professionally* uses, intellect—that is to say, the power "to know and to reason." The word "professionally" was intentionally stressed, for this seems to be the only defining element missing here. To make a daily search of knowledge through reasoning creates a habit or distortion that may become the specific difference that will finally characterize intellectuals. Were this so, consequences would be unsuspected; by way of example, it would be worth while to mention two. He who cultivates an art would have to be excluded from that class, for in this craft the intellectual tool is not used—at least, not predominantly. The other example would be that the intellectual cannot cease to have a critical disposition, since the simple rational statement of a problem leads him to ponder the possible solution that should be critically appraised. This, in turn, brings about an inevitable consequence: critical analysis requires time, and, while unfinished, the intellectual's attitude has to be one of hesitation or expectation.

To clarify, even to a reduced extent, the other term of the relation, politics, is a still more complex task; it seems that in our time each one holds his own idea of what politics is and, even, of what it should be.

Also found in the English dictionary is an innocent definition of politics as the "art of ruling and enacting laws and regulations to preserve peace and public security and to keep order and good customs." Of course, this one has the decisive flaw of not separating politics from administration. While no one questions the advisability or the need of the intellectual's intervention in administrative matters, doubts about making him a participant in politics arise by the dozen. But, even after separating administration, those concerned in the clarification of this problem would not accept such a definition, which presents, barely and in an awkward manner, a liberal philosophy that probably would not be recognized by even the most "classic" liberal. The goal of political action is much higher: to give all men as much material, moral, esthetic, and intellectual satisfaction as possible. Order, peace, public security—not to mention "good" customs—will be given in addition.

Here, however, two secondary defining elements are of particular interest. First, politics involves a continued action as well as a strategy and a policy fit for the management of public matters. Secondly, these reflections have to be generically restricted to Western society, and, specifically, to Mexican society. For that reason, at this point, it is relevant to recall George Bernard Shaw's remark when he launched himself into politics on the Fabians' side: "The politician that of yore had to learn to flatter the King, nowadays has to know how to fascinate, amuse, wheedle or otherwise awake the electorate's fantasy." Even though expressed in his inevitably paradoxical tone, Shaw's remark contains more than one truth: that a king has died and another king lives no more; that is to say, that the system of absolute monarchy is gone forever. As a matter of fact, not in vain has it been said that democracy is the government of the people, by the people, and for the people, or, in other words, that the people own the power, exercise it, and administer it for their own benefit. Likewise, it has not been accidental that written democratic constitutions mention that the people are the sole source of sovereignty, and for that same reason give the name of "sovereign" to the people, when the king was thus named in the past.

Shaw is also right when, as well as considering that the courtiers or "clique" politicians fit themselves to flatter the king to obtain his favors and the power derived from them, he speaks of the need to abandon the royal palace and go to the public plaza (so called because the people are there): it is there that the people should be flattered in order that their favor may be obtained. Finally, Shaw points out the change in the technique of flattery: first, it is necessary to endeavor to fascinate the people; if this cannot be done, efforts should be made to amuse them; and if support is not then forthcoming, the people should be wheedled, *i.e.,* beguiled. Fortunately, at the end of these three procedures, Shaw generalizes: ". . . or otherwise awake the electorate's fantasy." By substituting "fantasy" for "interest," we will tread on a less merry but firmer ground.

In short, in offering a whole series of techniques with which to conquer the people's esteem, Shaw is again right: the conquest of power involves the risk of failing in its management. Shaw was never solemn and had scant regard for any intelligence except his own; but the essence of his last sentence is equivalent to saying that it is worth while to run that risk for the sake of intelligence, for in that manner the immediate approval of the electorate and the distant one of history shall be accomplished.

Let us now examine the peculiar conditions wherein the life of politics in Mexico and that of the intellectuals within it have developed.

Of course, a significant series of factors has prevented democratic habits', rather than ideas', taking root in Mexico. Not even today can it be truthfully asserted that the government belongs to the people; nor can it be said that the people themselves exercise it, although throughout the government's independent life it has been said that its administration was for the people's benefit. This has actually been the case in a good many instances.

To begin with, we have geography. Granted that, compared with a few colossuses such as the United States, Brazil, and Canada in America, or China, India, and the Soviet Union in Asia, Mexico looks small, but its two million square kilometers of territory outmeasure the area of any European country and of most African, Asiatic, and American countries. The difficulty involved in an extensive territory is aggravated by its adverse topography: the country is crisscrossed in all directions by long, high mountain ranges; not only does it lack great plains, but its central part is reduced to an endless series of small valleys separated by high mountains. Physical communication, so significant for a uniform economical progress, and spiritual communication, so necessary for a nation's unity and government, have been difficult and costly.

Population is another serious obstacle. It has been low in relation to the magnitude of the territory, so that in the nineteenth century its density was scarcely ten inhabitants per square kilometer; at present, it is barely seventeen. More than its absolute number and density, its distribution should be considered. Throughout the nineteenth century, the rural population, *i.e.* those people living in communities with not more than 2,000 inhabitants, easily represented 80 per cent of the total; at present, despite a strong tendency toward urban concentration, notably accentuated in the past thirty years, it still represents 55 per cent. Hence, Mexican population is not only mainly rural, but, within that portion so classified by census, the great part lives in communities of not more than 1,000 inhabitants.

Because of the physical remoteness of such small groups from any government center, the numerous and varied facilities of modern living are unattainable and exceedingly expensive: those of a social, educational, and health nature; those of simple communication, such as electricity, railroads, highways, telegraph and telephone; and those involving entertainment, such as the cinema, radio, television, theaters, and museums. It is, then, no wonder that in the past forty years the rate of illiteracy has decreased from 55 per cent only to 29 per cent, in spite of vigorous campaigns for improvement.

To get a full, though very schematic, picture, two additional facts should be considered. First, pre-Colombian Indians did not belong to a single "race," but to many, so that anthropologists have identified over a hundred Indian tongues or dialects; second, even though it be granted that the Spanish soldier's mixing with the Mexican Indian women started from the very first day of the conquest, such mixing of races has not become as complete as in Chile. Racial prejudice has never existed in Mexico; even so, as a general rule rural population is less hybrid or more purely indigenous than urban population.

These two main circumstances, the geographical and the demographic, as well as a thousand others of a secondary and different nature, have given Mexico peculiar and strong features which, however, lack a unique originality. On the one hand, reference can rightly be made to a traditional and even archaic rural community, whose stability at times seems immovable; on the other hand, there is an ultramodern, fluid, and changing urban community. To that double social structure one may compare an economy which is also dual: predominantly agricultural and, until recently, autarchic even as it is an economy of trade, commercial and industrial, and of utilities. It may also be assumed that a relation exits between those situations and the country's general political style.

The juridical-constitutional scheme has usually been inspired in a unique community, which is homogeneous and possesses urban, commercial, and industrial characteristics; therefore, the distance between the wording and even the meaning of the constitutional text and its actual, practical application has always been remarkable. This has brought about such incalculable consequences as the general skepticism with which legal redress is viewed and the resulting desire to seek the actual solution, the only one deemed really effective; an everlasting inclination to try a new law, since the previous one failed to give the desired results; and the readiness with which the flouted law becomes a revolutionary vindication, and so on.

Another phenomenon which merits attention is that the government and the administration, excessively present in the large city, lose vigor and efficiency when applied to smaller and more distant communities. Hence the coexistence in them of a *de facto* authority (generally known as the political boss) and a *de jure* authority (mostly theoretical), from the large urban center (whether the country's capital, seat of the national government, or the state's capital), where the strongest local power has its seat.

DANIEL COSIO VILLEGAS

Even in the most democratic country, it may be said, the people do not directly exercise power; on their behalf, it is applied by representatives whom they elect, so that masses are always governed by a group who are selected, chosen, or elected. Of course, the same is true of Mexico, but, literally, even more so. Such an imperfect integration of rural population and even of lower urban classes into the daily political active life turns it into a mass that is rather mineral than human. The nucleus that holds the actual political power is so small, so urban-minded and, consequently, so distant from the actual human being it pretends to rule, that it forms an *elite* in the most aristocratic sense of the word. This, added to the circumstances mentioned above and the fact that active politics, and therefore its anticipated success, is concentrated in the great urban crowd, results at once in the retention there of many government and administration benefits, with few or none reaching the rural areas. In turn, this neglect of the country creates a potentially explosive element; now and then this flares up, whether through the conjurations of an "agitator" or at the instigation of city politicians connected with, or pretending to be connected with, rural interests.

The awakening of rural masses turns, many times, into violent revolutionary explosions that are local or general, temporary or of a more extended duration, and with theoretical goals and actual accomplishments that vary widely in meaning and durability. At times, the masses are satisfied with the suspension of an administrative ruling or repeal of a certain regulation or secondary law, or with the replacement of a local authority. At other times, the protest or revolt extends over a whole province or even the entire nation.

In the face of such political disturbances, the Mexican intellectual's position has changed according to the nature, extension, depth, and persistence of the disturbances; but, even so, history teaches that almost never has the intellectual been the material, or even the ideological, initiator of those disturbances; very seldom has he been the distant animator of them, or even an important personality. His participation was indefinite when disturbances occurred in connection with an international war (in 1846–1848 against the United States, or in 1862–1867 against England, Spain, and France), and its only definite evidence was in the single case of a controversy (which resulted in general civil war) whose justification (and even its very name) represented an ideological difference: the prolonged disagreement between liberals and conservatives that reached its zenith in the period from 1854 to 1867.

The best example of intellectuals' participation—because of its importance and its recency—is to be found in the Mexican Revolution, a truly revolutionary movement which, from 1910 through 1920, swept away the "old regime" and from 1920 to 1940 built up an entirely new society. The contribution of the Mexican intellectual to the Revolution's ideology is amazingly limited in quality and efficiency. A part of it had a touch of moral value because it became evident (through daily or weekly periodicals) when the tyrannical government of Porfirio Díaz was still strong enough to punish his opponents with cruelty; but its ideological significance was scarce, since it did not even offer an accurate radiograph of the Díaz regime, much less an attractive picture of the new society which the country could, and should, eagerly desire. Its other contribution—the most persistent and, in a way, the most "revolutionary—had a higher moral value and a certain ideological significance, despite its origin in a not very select reading of the anarchist literature which was very popular at the time; but it was not a determinant factor in the trend followed by the Revolution.

Precisely because of the absence of patterns or of an ideological inspiration, the Mexican Revolution is frequently spoken of as a spontaneous popular movement, born, so to speak, of nothing, or—more correctly—springing out of the Mexican soil. The same may be truly said if consideration is given to the people's physical contribution to the armed victory, and especially if the function and social origin of the leaders are considered. Of course, for many years—say, from 1913 through 1924—they all participated actively, as military chiefs rather than political leaders, and this in itself marked an abundant contribution on the part of the intellectuals. But this was very much limited by the circumstance that most of those leaders came from the country and not from cities. If it is true that, with the exception of Villa and Zapata, the national leaders belonged to the middle class (Madero, Carranza, Obregón, Calles, and Cárdenas), it cannot be assumed even remotely that they were intellectuals: they read little and wrote less and had hardly finished their primary education. On the contrary, all could be regarded, albeit in notably different degrees, as anti-intellectuals.

More than anything else, the Mexican Revolution was a movement devoted to the destruction of the authority of Porfirio Díaz, not only because it was arbitrary and tyrannical but also because it was centrally applied from Mexico City, the country's great metropolis; it was, as well, directed against the subordinate but no less centralized and arbitrary authority of the state or provincial governor and the district's political mayor. For that single reason, the Revolution was to a large extent actually a movement of the country against the city, of the groups that were less favored by the Díaz government against the most favored ones.

To the fact that intellectuals lived essentially in the city was added a mere historical coincidence. Porfirio Díaz, who throughout his life suffered a severe intellectual allergy, had about him, during the last fifteen years of his regime, a group of counselors who were not authentic intellectuals but who, calling themselves "scientists," claimed to be such intelligent and learned men that they could scientifically run the country—that is to say, rule it by purely rational standards. Much of the people's hatred of Porfirio Díaz was concentrated on the group composed of these "scientists" to the extent that many thought that without them Díaz would have been a fair ruler.

No wonder the revolutionary leaders distrusted intellectuals! Furthermore—and without any regard to past events—those leaders had so much confidence in themselves that they thought they understood their goals and how to attain them, that they had very little need of information and advice that the intellectuals could have provided. And perhaps for that reason, in spite of their lack of rational and technical training and the fact that many of them were not innately intelligent, they themselves and alone created a new Mexico which without doubt is much better than the old one.

DANIEL COSIO VILLEGAS

Further, to the intellectual's despair, the Mexican Revolution proved to have a worthy ideological origin.

That divorce between arms and letters could, of course, not last forever, nor even for long, despite the fact that at no time was it ever absolute. The greater the rudeness of the revolutionary soldier, the greater was his need of a world-magician, a man with the ability to express himself verbally and, more important, in writing, and thus to communicate ideas. It was, for instance, undeferably urgent to draw up the revolutionary "plan," the *cahier de doleances* of the chief and the remedies for redressing the denounced evils. But, at the same time, there always existed a certain affinity between the chief and his amanuensis. Unlearned chiefs, like Emiliano Zapata, if at all, enjoyed the benefits of simple rural professors; the literature they produced was less elaborate but perhaps more sincere. Carranza was assisted by Luis Cabrera, a young lawyer who proved to be an intelligent man, a good debater and a better book collector, and, in the last years of his life, a painstaking linguist. Villa, who was, like Zapata, ignorant, and, unlike Zapata, rude, had in his army Martín Luis Guzmán and José Vasconcelos, two members of the already famous "Ateneo de la Juventud," who, when mature, became two of the greatest writers of Modern Mexico and who more than qualified, therefore, to be regarded as "intellectuals."

In truth, however, it is well to state that intellectuals allied to revolutionary leaders were not very numerous and that their influence was exceedingly limited. It may certainly be said that Martín Luis Guzmán and José Vasconcelos failed to instill in Villa any idea or plan; it is even more questionable that Villa ever consulted them on even unimportant questions. Luis Cabrera was closer to Carranza, but his greatest influence was exerted, not in his chief's revolutionary days but when Carranza had become the constitutional president. Most civilians who approached the revolutionary leaders were, of a certainty, persons who could read and write—like newspapermen—or who could draw up regulations and even laws—like lawyers—or the agronomy student and the agronomist, whose services became essential when the old, large estates were first divided and distributed among farmers.

Thus, it may be stated that, except for José Vasconcelos (first as president of the National University of Mexico and later as Secretary of Education from 1920 to 1924), none of the Mexican intellectuals enjoyed the full confidence of a revolutionary chief; none had political power, direct or otherwise, as evidenced by the fact that Vasconcelos became, soon after, a strong candidate for the presidency of the Republic.

But the situation has apparently changed since the Revolution began, in 1940, to be "institutional," and particularly so during the last eighteen or twenty years. Lázaro Cárdenas was the last military leader to reach the presidency (1934–40); Manuel Ávila Camacho succeeded him but had, in the army, performed only administrative work (1940–46); of the four succeeding presidents (1946 to the present), three were lawyers—that is to say, university men. Not only is this true but, in these same years, a kind of tradition has been established that the Secretary of Public Health be a doctor, the Secretary of Public Works, a civil engineer, the Secretary of Communications, a mechanical-electrical engineer, the Secretary of Industry and Commerce, an economist, the Secretary of Foreign Affairs, a career diplomat, and the Secretary of Agriculture, an agronomist, and so on.

This might give the impression that present political life in Mexico is a sort of Platonic Republic or an intellectuals' paradise. It so happens, however, that in this connection there are either equivocal situations or more external appearance than reality.

It seems beyond all doubt that *middle sectors*—as with deliberate vagueness, Stanford's Professor Johnson calls them—or middle class, as mentioned above, in present-day Mexico have an influence never before exerted; hence without much risk of error it may be stated that the main resources of the entire life of this country—political, economic, social, and cultural, both official and private—are in the hands of a middle class, newly formed or lacking old traditions but, in any case well defined. Although the intellectual, as a general rule, comes from the middle class, it is hardly necessary to add that not all members of that class are intellectuals. Nor, necessarily, are professionals (physicians, lawyers, economists, engineers, or agronomists); conversely, it would be more nearly true to state that, provided the reverse is not proved, professionals should not be considered as intellectuals.

But what really counts is this: professionals who are so prominently participating in so many and such outstanding official assignments have been asked to cooperate as technicians and not, by any means, as politicians, *i.e.* they participate in the administration, but not in the country's government. To emphasize this point further, their duty is to perform the politics outlined and the decisions taken by the President of the Republic, who is the sole responsible authority, both juridically and actually, of all the acts of the executive power, the only one, on the other hand, of the three powers that has predominance in national life.

Does this mean that such technocrats are deprived of all political power, or that they dislike it and do not seek it? They absolutely lack a primary or original power that is, as just stated, held only by the President of the Republic who may, according to the Constitution, "nominate and dismiss" them freely—that is to say, according to his whim. But, while they enjoy the president's confidence, their derived, or secondary, power is always significant. Naturally, they have a firsthand knowledge of all matters brought to their ministries or departments by other government agencies, by private institutions, or by any private citizen. Although all of these constantly have available the second and last resource of the president, they prefer to remain at the first resource if the anticipated settlement of their problem is likely to favor them. Furthermore, technocrats submit to the superior resolution of the president a large number of important matters; of course, in so doing, they may act disloyally—that is, not in line with the country's best interests but according to whimsical or egotistic opinions—and it is likely that, more often than not, they present the matter in such a manner as to flatter the president's vanity or power.

DANIEL COSIO VILLEGAS

It seems to me that a single question now calls for an explanation: why does the Mexican intellectual fail to participate actively in politics? This failure exists in spite of his eager desire to participate and, also, despite the fact that present-day conditions appear to provide an excellent opportunity to do so. The explanation, of course, is complex, but part of it may be found in causes beyond the intellectual's power; the balance will be found within himself.

In the first place, the influence of the government on the national life is tremendous, for there are seldom any segments of activity, independent or even distant, that do not come under that influence. Such being the case, any public activity immediately confronts that giant of excessive strength. It is possible, therefore, to make some politics *within* and in favor of the government, but to make it facing or *opposing* it would be equivalent to undertaking a useless activity. The chances of attaining power not just in defiance of the government, but not even on its side, are thus remote, not to say nil. Obviously, neither the Mexican intellectual nor any rational being wishes to play the role of a martyr or of a preacher in the desert.

The only exception recorded in the recent history of our country is that of Manuel Gómez Morín, initiator and supporter for ten long years of the opposition party, Acción Nacional. This exception is remarkable for its uniqueness and because it may offer all Mexican intellectuals a substance that merits the most serious consideration. It proves beyond doubt that a passionate interest and stubborn effort may give birth to a political party that is, if not openly opposed to the government, at least alien to it. Unfortunately, no definite conclusion is reached concerning two basic facts. One is the extent to which that result depended upon the fact that Acción Nacional placed itself on the right wing of a government that labels itself "revolutionary." Gauging of the second fact proves impossible, and it is even risky to speculate on it. Would not Manuel Gómez Morín have been more useful to his country by working within the government? This would not have been impossible or even difficult had he been more patient and had the Mexican governments that let him go been more conscious of what they would lose by his absence.

Secondly, revolutionary governments have somehow managed to continue the identification of any reform with the "dogma" of the Mexican Revolution, that is, with something which is beyond any doubt. Moreover, they have managed things in such a way as immediately to stick the label of "reactionary" on all sorts of opponents, or even on the simple questioning about the need of such reforms. And the Mexican intellectual, generally pleased by his country's achievements and also conscious that change is the sign of today's world, does not care to appear as favoring retrogression or even stagnation.

There is also another circumstance, daughter of an omnipotent government, that injures the intellectual, and this is the fashion—let us call it so—peculiar to political life throughout the prolonged dictatorship of Porfirio Díaz (1877–1911) and also extant for about the last thirty years: politics is not made at the public plaza, at the parliament or by newspapers, at sensational debates or controversies, but through direct conversation, in softly spoken words, between the power-hunter and the man who has power. It is not therefore, a public activity, but rather a confidential whisper. Words, gestures, cries, and, of course, ideas, amount to little; what is decisive is the insinuation—letting fall the bitter drop at the right moment. The question is not, as stated by George Bernard Shaw, to attract the public's attention but to court a president who is actually a king; politics, therefore, is courtier intrigue and the confrontation of divergent solutions to the country's problems. This peculiar style of making politics involves two fatal consequences for the intellecual. On the one hand, it prevents his using intellectual and oral expression—that is, his best weapons—and compels him to resort to intrigue, which means to convince by deceit and not by reason.

As though this were not enough, the Mexican intellectual confronts still another adverse situation that prevails all over the world and whose influence, of course, it is impossible for him to elude: the function of the intellectual and the function of the politician are very different. Among other things, they require, if not a different personal disposition and training, at least the use of so dissimilar techniques that any intellectual who enters politics performs within it with the uncertainty and clumsiness with which a sailfish would play tennis.

Nonetheless it may be asserted that if the Mexican intellectual does not actually make politics, it is to a large extent his own fault, for he has failed to prove his ability to offer many original ideas on national problems; still less does he hold such ideas as true convictions, that is, to the extent that he is willing to defend and impose them, or, in extreme cases, to sacrifice himself for them. Even though lacking intelligence and imagination, his political action would have some meaning if it had a visible moral strength, capable of winning the public's good will. Consider, for instance, that daily handling of the revolutionary "dogma" which stops all the critical intent of government measures. If the intellectual at no time resolves to challenge, openly and publicly, the supposedly untouchable nature of that revolutionary dogma; if he does not decide to proclaim his opposition to any of these measures because he finds them useless or detrimental, without being concerned that, because of his attitude, he is most conspicuously branded as a reactionary, it is evident that his political activity will not amount to much. As a matter of fact, he should realize that, for the time being, everything—or almost everything—is against him and that, consequently, more than immediately showing his hand in the political game, he should initiate the necessarily slow task of radically transforming the environment in which he is now condemned to live to the extent of making it favorable to an intelligent political action.

DANIEL COSIO VILLEGAS

FRANCISCO MIRÓ QUESADA : *El Intelectual en la Política Occidental*

EL CONCEPTO DE INTELECTUAL

EN GENERAL LOS TÉRMINOS QUE SE EMPLEAN PARA HABLAR SOBRE ASUNTOS humanos son poco precisos. El término "intelectual" no escapa a esta limitación. Empero, es imprescindible utilizarlo, en todo lo que sigue, con el mayor rigor posible, pues si se utiliza indiscriminadamente se corre el peligro de hacer planteamientos tan vagos que hagan imposible una discusión fecunda.

Los términos que no pertenecen a las ciencias exactas tienen un núcleo y una penumbra significativa. Es muy útil en casos como el presente limitar el intento de rigorización al núcleo. Porque con frecuencia es posible esclarecer luego aspectos importantes de la penumbra.

Es indudable que el núcleo significativo del término "intelectual" contiene la dedicación a las disciplinas cognoscitivas. Es posible que la extensión del término abarque actividades tan distintas como la del periodista, el poeta, el profesional liberal, el ideólogo, el maestro, etc. Pero es indudable que aquellas personas cuya principal actividad es la dedicación sistemática al conocimiento, son intelectuales. O sea, el filósofo y el científico, tal como los concibe nuestra Cultura Occidental son intelectuales, porque la filosofía y la ciencia son disciplinas eminentemente cognoscitivas. La actividad científica y la filosófica, pertenecen al centro mismo del núcleo significativo del término. También pertenecen al núcleo significativo la asimilación de conocimientos y la trasmisión de conocimientos. Una persona dedicada a la adquisición de conocimientos, o a la enseñanza de los mismos, es considerada casi siempre como intelectual. Pero ya aquí la evidencia no es tan grande, porque interviene una especie de grado cualitativo en la determinación de la pertenencia a la extensión. Por ejemplo, un brillante maestro universitario que no sea un investigador, es sin lugar a dudas un intelectual; pero un maestro primario, que enseña las primeras letras, no es considerado, en general, como intelectual.

El caso del arte es ambiguo. Para muchos, los artistas son intelectuales. Mas, para otros no lo son. Algunos consideran que los poetas, los novelistas y los dramaturgos son intelectuales porque emplean la palabra escrita, pero que los demás artistas no lo son.

Para alcanzar el máximo rigor en la exposición, nos limitaremos al centro mismo del núcleo: los filósofos y los científicos. Al hablar de intelectuales entenderemos aquellas personas dedicadas a la práctica de la filosofía y de la ciencia en toda su extensión, desde las matemáticas hasta la historia. Los demás casos, los dejaremos a la elección de los interlocutores.

EL INTELECTUAL Y EL OCCIDENTE

Para comprender la relación del intelectual con la política en Occidente es necesario remontarse al origen de la Cultura Occidental. Porque se trata de una relación constitutiva, y este tipo de relaciones se ven con mayor nitidez a través de los procesos históricos. La Cultura Occidental se forma a través de un largo proceso que culmina en el Renacimiento con la eclosión de una primera toma de conciencia. En el Renacimiento se aglutina una constelación de vigencias que son las que constituyen el ethos del hombre occidental. Estas vigencias son varias, pero es indudable que entre ellas, en primerísimo rango, se halla *la creencia en la eficacia de la razón*. Para el occidental la razón es una facultad suprema, que le permite resolver problemas de todo tipo (tanto teóricos como prácticos) de manera segura. La razón es la facultad del convencimiento, hace posible la actividad *suasoria* de los hombres. Cuando el occidental es capaz de presentar la prueba racional de algo, siente que todos deben quedar convencidos. La prueba racional tiene la característica de que, cuando puede hacerse, es el criterio último de decisión. No hay, para el occidental, ningún tribunal superior donde se pueda apelar.

El origen lejano de esta vigencia es el ideal de racionalidad planteado por un pequeño grupo de filósofos griegos. Los filósofos griegos son los primeros en utilizar a la razón como criterio de decisión para resolver los grandes problemas teóricos y prácticos del hombre. Frente a los criterios augurales o tradicionalistas empleados por las otras culturas y por la propia cultura helénica, proponen el ejercicio de la razón. Es importante observar que, aunque los griegos descubren el significado de la razón, la cultura griega nunca tuvo el ideal de racionalidad como vigencia constitutiva. En la Hélade, los ejércitos, cuando iniciaban la guerra jamás cruzaban la frontera del país enemigo si los resultados del augurio no eran propicios. En la época en que Sócrates filosofaba por las calles de Atenas, el criterio supremo de decisión empleado por los griegos era el augurio. Pero a pesar de que la cultura helénica no tuvo entre sus vigencias constitutivas el ideal de racionalidad, los filósofos griegos fueron los primeros que lo plantearon. Descubrieron que el hombre poseía en sí mismo un poder incomparable, un poder que no podía ser vencido por ninguna fuerza ni divina ni humana: la razón. Los resultados del conocimiento racional se imponían a todas las inteligencias cualquiera que fuera la época en que vivieran y la región donde habitaran. Mientras las diversas religiones y costumbres del orbe se oponían de manera irreconciliable, la razón era una sola y unía a todos los hombres.

Platón formula con toda precisión el ideal del conocimiento racional. La razón parte de evidencias cognoscitivas, que se captan de manera necesaria y universal, que se imponen a todas las mentes y que son comunicables. Y de ellas deriva una sucesión inagotable de conocimientos. Mediante este procedimiento debe ser posible conocer todos los aspectos de la realidad. No sólo la manera como es la realidad sino también como debe ser. Así como la razón capta los principios supremos de los números o de las formas, así también capta los principios supremos de la acción, nos dice qué cosas debemos hacer y qué cosas no debemos hacer. De aquí se deriva el ideal de *sociedad racional o sociedad justa*, en donde todos los hombres viven una vida regida por los principios de la razón. Se constituye así el *ideal de vida racional*, es decir, de una vida en la que todas las grandes decisiones pueden fundarse en el conocimiento racional, en que la razón es el criterio que permite a los hombres entenderse entre ellos y resolver sus problemas de acuerdo a principios que nadie puede discutir, porque son la esencia misma del espíritu humano.

Este ideal confiere una dignidad nueva al hombre, Le hace comprender que nadie, por más poderoso que sea, puede cambiar los principios de la razón. Cualquier hombre, en cambio, por más humilde que sea puede enmendar a otro hombre si éste ha cometido error en el empleo de la razón. Por eso el hombre mide su grandeza, no por el poder material sino por la adecuación de sus actos a las normas de la razón. Además, todos los hombres poseen razón. Por mayores que sean las diferencias que existen entre los individuos, hay algo que constituye su esencia, que es la razón y que es igual en todos. Una humanidad nueva, capaz de alcanzar verdades necessarias y universales para todos sus miembros, con una unidad totalmente desconocida hasta entonces, con una dignidad más alta, con una capacidad de decisión y una autonomía avasalladoras. He aquí el hombre forjándose a sí mismo a través de una historia, guiado por la meta de la vida racional.

Mediante un proceso aún no suficientemente estudiado, este ideal de vida racional comienza a trasformarse en vigencia durante la Edad Media. Al lado de otras vigencias, como los valores cristianos, el nacionalismo, el trabajo como poder, el ideal de vida racional va tomando cada vez más cuerpo. Asumida en un principio por ciertas elites intelectuales de las ciudades-estado italianas se va difundiendo con fuerza arrolladora por todo Occidente. A mediados del siglo XVII se ha trasformado en la vigencia fundamental. Los hombres se dedican al conocimiento por la satisfacción que les proporciona el ejercicio de la razón, y en todas las clases, desde la aristocracia hasta las masas populares, los argumentos racionales comienzan a tener la última palabra. Cada vez más, los argumentos científicos comienzan a imponerse por su carácter racional. Logran imponerse incluso contra creencias basadas en la tradición y las convicciones religiosas. Los filósofos comienzan a hablar sobre la mejor manera de organizar la sociedad y a hacer profundos análisis sobre las fuentes del poder. Llegan a la conclusión de que las vigencias tradicionales sobre el origen del poder no tienen fundamento racional y los grupos dominantes se ven obligados a asumir actitudes de fuerza contra los intelectuales que difunden estos puntos de vista, por el temor que produce su inexorable poder suasorio. Cada vez más, es la razón la que se emplea como criterio de decisión en los asuntos importantes y cada vez que hay conflicto entre la razón y otras vigencias se impone la razón. Después de las guerras de religión sólo el nacionalismo parece tener una vigencia tan acendrada. Es la única fuerza capaz de impulsar a los grandes grupos humanos mediante la utilización de criterios no racionales.

La Ilustración es la culminación de esta ascensión hacia la razón que caracteriza a Occidente. Los enciclopedistas son los primeros en crear una *ideología* como justificación filosófica de la praxis política. Pero ya desde Hobbes, Bacon y luego Locke, el occidental comienza a hacer uso del análisis racional para resolver los problemas sociales y encontrar normas para la praxis política. El ideal de vida racional en la praxis política, encuentra su exponente más alto en la admirable obra del barón d'Holbach, *La politique naturelle*. El subtítulo lo dice todo: *Discours sur les vrais principes du gouvernement*. Los filósofos de la "Encyclopedie," en vísperas de la revolución, que ellos han contribuido a poner en marcha, anuncian el hermoso amanecer de una nueva humanidad, la alborada de los hombres libres cuya vida sólo se rige por los principios supremos de la razón.

FILOSOFÍA Y POLÍTICA

Las anteriores consideraciones muestran la profunda relación que existe entre el intelectual y la política en la cultura de Occidente. Si el ideal de vida racional es una de las vigencias constitutivas de dicha cultura, probablemente la más central y determinante, y sus alcances se extienden a la totalidad de la actividad humana, es evidente que la política—una de las más importantes actividades del hombre—debe caer bajo su ámbito. Si el hombre de Occidente se afana por racionalizar su mundo, es natural que uno de sus principales afanes sea la racionalización de su vida política. Esta racionalización ha correspondido tradicionalmente a la filosofía. O sea, el intelectual (o si se quiere, uno de los tipos más importantes de intelectual que existe en Occidente) es el llamado a proporcionar los fundamentos racionales de la política. Por eso, la filosofía occidental, casi desde sus comienzos, principia a meditar sobre la esencia de la sociedad y la mejor manera de organizarla. Y desde mediados del siglo XVIII, cuando el ideal de vida racional ha calado ya hasta el fondo mismo de Occidente, comienzan a nacer los movimientos políticos explícitamente fundados en principios filosóficos, comienza a nacer la *política ideológica*. Desde esta época hasta el presente todos los grandes movimientos políticos se han basado siempre en una filosofía, es decir han tenido *ideología*. La política y la filosofía han constituído en Occidente una relación esencial y característica. Nuestra cultura se diferencia en esto de todas las demás, incluso de la helénica, que concibió la posibilidad de racionalizar la política e incluso inició el proceso teórico de racionalización, pero nunca produjo movimientos políticos teóricamente fundados.

LAS LIMITACIONES INTRÍNSECAS DE LA RAZÓN Y EL DRAMA DE LA CULTURA OCCIDENTAL

Pero en el momento mismo en que Occidente alcanza el zenit de su ascensión hacia la razón, se encuentra ante un abismo en que todo parece precipitarse sin remedio. En el momento en que el hombre de Occidente comienza a organizar sus movimientos políticos sobre bases racionales, la filosofía racionalista comienza a desmoronarse. El movimiento racionalista que culmina en el enciclopedismo, tenía una fe ingenua en la posibilidad de realizar el ideal de racionalidad que había impulsado la ciencia y la filosofía desde el Renacimiento. Durante dos siglos los europeos creyeron que era posible captar mediante evidencias indubitables ciertas verdades eternas e inconmovibles y derivar de ellas, por medio de leyes lógicas igualmente evidentes, todo un sistema de verdades que permitiese el conocimiento global de la realidad y el encauzamiento ético de la acción humana. Pero he aquí que, debido al mismo avance de la filosofía y de la ciencia, a un avance realizado mediante los propios métodos del racionalismo, se comienza a comprender que el ideal racionalista es insostenible.

Desde que la filosofía en Grecia plantea el ideal racionalista, se esgrimen objeciones sumamente profundas. Pero a pesar de ellas el conocimiento racional comienza a organizarse y a avanzar con una seguridad que desconcierta a los escépticos. La constitución de la matemática y de la astronomía como ciencias rigurosas constituyen prueba plena de la posibilidad de la razón de llegar a conocimientos absolutos. Las dificultades que se encuentran en el propio campo de la matemática y en el conocimiento de otras regiones de la realidad, se interpretan como exigencias metodológicas difíciles de cumplir, pero realizables en principio. El progreso constante de las ciencias permite sostener este punto de vista y considerar el conocimiento racional como un proceso infinito, que avanza poco a poco en medio de dificultades innumerables, pero que de manera segura va conquistando la totalidad del mundo.

Kant muestra que el ideal racionalista, tal como se había planteado desde Descartes, es insostenible. El romanticismo alemán, hace un esfuerzo desesperado para recuperar la fe en la capacidad sin límites de la razón. Pero la filosofía de Hegel se parte en mil pedazos. El abismo se va haciendo cada vez más hondo. No sólo en la filosofía, sino en la ciencia, es decir en el campo en donde la razón ha logrado avanzar con mayor seguridad, el ideal racionalista comienza a resquebrajarse. El advenimiento de las geometrías no euclideanas significa que el ideal racionalista no puede sostenerse en geometría. Las paradojas de la teoría de los conjuntos muestran que no puede mantenerse ni siquiera en el campo que parecía representar de manera más directa y definitiva a la razón: la lógica. La crisis de la física clásica, el surgimiento de lógicas no aristotélicas, la posibilidad de construir diversos sistemas de principios derivativos, todo ello debilita la convicción de que existe un sistema de la razón en el que los conocimientos se fundan en evidencias de valor absoluto que permiten la conquista progresiva y sin término, pero sin retroceso, de la totalidad de la realidad. El surgimiento de ideologías diferentes, basadas en doctrinas filosóficas incompatibles contribuye a crear la impresión de que no es posible encontrar una solución racional de los problemas humanos. La Cultura Occidental corre el peligro de captarse a sí misma como una cultura frustrada, como un proyecto colectivo fundado en un ideal imposible.

LA CRISIS DE LA RAZÓN COMO UNA DEPURACIÓN DEL IDEAL RACIONALISTA

(a) Crisis de la ciencia y reajuste metodológico. Sin embargo la conclusión a la que llegan algunos pensadores y políticos occidentales sobre la imposibilidad de realizar el ideal de vida racional, es precipitada. Porque el hecho de no poder realizar el ideal de vida racional de manera perfecta no significa de ninguna manera que tengamos que echarlo por la borda. La historia muestra que si bien es cierto que la filosofía no ha podido encontrar un sistema evidente de valores que permitan encauzar la praxis humana de manera precisa, la razón ha tenido éxitos sorprendentes y ha avanzado un largo trecho en su esfuerzo por racionalizar el mundo.

En primer lugar la ciencia positiva, o sea *la filosofía que ha encontrado una metodología segura,* ha seguido avanzando de manera continua y ampliando su radio de acción a campos que, hace apenas pocos años, parecían inconquistables. La crisis de la ciencia muestra que la razón no es ni tan perfecta ni tan poderosa como creyeron los racionalistas clásicos. Pero no significa de ninguna manera que la ciencia no pueda

FRANCISCO MIRÓ QUESADA

constituirse como disciplina racional. Si se analizan cuidadosamente las crisis del pensamiento racional, se ve de inmediato que toda conclusión negativa se basa en una conclusión positiva. La crisis de la matemática y de la lógica se produce porque se lleva hasta sus últimas consecuencias las exigencias del ideal racionalista. Así las geometrías no euclideanas surgen, porque se demuestra que la eliminación o el cambio del V postulado de Euclides no conduce a contradicciones. O sea, que es la evidencia del principio de no contradicción, lo que permite mostrar que la evidencia de las formas espaciales no es, como se creía, absoluta. Y lo mismo sucede con la crisis de la lógica y de las matemáticas. La limitación del principio del tercio excluído, se descubre en el intento de encontrar una prueba de la consistencia da la aritmética formalizada, o sea, partiendo de la base de que el principio de no contradicción es indubitable. En ambos casos, como se ve, la crisis se produce porque se parte de un principio—el de contradicción—que es tan evidente y absoluto que no puede ser puesto en duda. Tanto en la construcción de las nuevas geometrías, como en la de los nuevos sistemas matemáticos abstractos, se utilizan diversos principios captados de manera intuitiva, de cuya evidencia no puede dudarse. Además, los diversos sistemas lógicos que difieren entre sí por el empleo de principios diferentes, presentan rasgos comunes, de los cuales no pueden prescindir, como el principio antifásico y el principio deductivo.

En las ciencias físicas, la situación es exactamenta la misma. La física clásica entra en crisis porque la evidencia del principio explicativo impone que todos los hechos observados queden explicados por la teoría vigente. La pérdida de vigencia de las evidencias clásicas sobre el tiempo y el espacio y del principio de causalidad, se deben a la evidencia incontrastable de que una teoría física debe explicar los hechos.

El análisis del proceso de las grandes crisis de la ciencia nos descubre así, algo que no puede comprenderse sino dentro del propio racionalismo. Las crisis se producen porque ciertas evidencias racionales son tan fuertes, que se hace necesario "sacrificar" otras evidencias para mantener la vigencia de las primeras. La razón exhibe, así, al análisis, cierto dinamismo orientado por un vector, cierto movimiento hacia una depuración de sus evidencias. Esto permite pensar que, a través de un proceso histórico, la razón va constituyendo un sistema de evidencias por medio de una selección, utilizando un criterio que aún debe ser esclarecido. Pero la tesis del colapso de la razón debido a sus limitaciones intrínsecas, no puede sostenerse de ninguna manera. En síntesis, el proceso puede describirse como una depuración del sistema de la razón a través de un proceso dentro de la propia razón. Todas las crisis y limitaciones de la razón, se han producido porque se han aplicado ciertos métodos de análisis racional, de cuya validez no puede dudarse. Las limitaciones descubiertas, son indubitables, porque se han revelado a través de ciertos principios que son también indubitables. Y estos principios, que se van revelando a través de un dinamismo sui géneris, constituyen un complejo de validez suprahistórica.

Además, el hecho de que *toda* la matemática no pueda fundarse de manera absoluta, no le resta valor como ciencia. La matemática conserva todo su valor, porque, aunque teóricamente no puede demostrarse que *toda* ella se basa en evidencias absolutas, en la práctica, puede suponerse que está teóricamente saneada. Y lo mismo puede decirse de la ciencia física. Por eso, últimamente, el método matemático ha avanzado en sus conquistas de manera asombrosa, haciendo posible el análisis racional de ciertos aspectos de la vida social. Y no parece haber límites definidos para este avance.

(b) La filosofía como técnica del desenmascaramiento. Por otra parte, la tradición filosófica de Occidente se desarrolla a través de un enfrentamiento con las vigencias sociales imperantes. Si bien es cierto que la filosofía ha sido incapaz de elaborar un sistema completo que permita determinar con evidencia incuestionable la estructura de la sociedad racional, es innegable que, en sus análisis críticos ha logrado resultados incontrovertibles. Una vez planteado el ideal de vida racional, una vez proclamado el ideal de organizar la sociedad sobre bases racionales, la filosofía muestra, a través de un proceso histórico de vastas dimensiones, que ninguno de los sistemas imperantes puede considerarse racional. Para que la praxis social sea considerada racional, debe fundarse en evidencias universales, y ninguno de los sistemas sociales históricos que encuentran los filósofos racionalistas, presenta estos caracteres. La filosofía, inicia, así, una labor de crítica, que después de un proceso de extraordinaria pugnacidad, termina para siempre con las vigencias que permitían sostener los regímenes arbitrarios de las diversas monarquías occidentales. A través de un movimiento que se inicia en Bacon y que culmina en la filosofía de la Ilustración, la filosofía *desenmascara* los falsos fundamentos de los regímenes imperantes.

Pero esta función de desenmascaramiento no termina con el derrumbamiento de los regímenes monárquicos. La labor de crítica sigue su curso y se enraiza cada vez más en el espíritu de Occidente. El socialismo y el marxismo desenmascaran ciertos aspectos de las democracias liberales, y la filosofía occidental moderna desenmascara los errores del marxismo. La experiencia histórica de Occidente permite afirmar que la filosofía ha desbaratado teóricamente todos los sistemas sociales que han pretendido ser el fundamento de la sociedad justa. Y en este aspecto, no puede decirse que la razón haya fracasado por completo. Es cierto que ha fracasado en el intento positivo, o sea, en la forjación de un sistema definitivo de la praxis social. Pero ha triunfado ampliamente en el aspecto negativo: en la crítica de todos los sistemas arbitrarios que han sido utilizados por los grupos dominantes para justificar su posición de dominio.

(c) El fracaso de las filosofías y el triunfo de la razón. Las anteriores consideraciones muestran que la impresión de frustración que produjo la crisis de la ciencia en un momento dado, se debió a la dificultad de interpretar un proceso que se ha desarrollado dentro de los propios cauces del conocimiento racional. La crisis fue el producto del progreso en los métodos de análisis empleados por la misma razón. Las mayores exigencias de rigor, la posibilidad de acercarse cada vez más al ideal de rigor ínsito en todo ideal racional, fue lo que produjo un cambio en las concepciones clásicas. Pero debido a la tendencia humana a permanecer en las vigencias imperantes, es que se consideró que la razón había sido herida de muerte.

Sin embargo, después de la crisis, el ideal de racionalidad constitutivo de la Cultura Occidental, emerge más nítido y vigente que nunca. La crisis de la ciencia y de la lógica no ha detenido el progreso de la ciencia. La matemática ha logrado un rigor jamás igualado y ha encontrado principios de evidencia inconmovible (aunque no con la amplitud que esperaba el racionalismo clásico), la física ha ingresado en una etapa más amplia y fecunda que la clásica, las ciencias sociales han conquistado campos increíbles. El progreso del conocimiento racional ha permitido crear una técnica que hace posible racionalizar cada vez más la circundancia humana.

Es cierto que los sistemas filosóficos a través de la historia han ido adquiriendo y perdiendo vigencia uno después del otro. Es cierto también que ninguno de ellos ha logrado elaborar un sistema social que haya resistido la crítica de los sistemas rivales. Pero también es cierto que la filosofía ha contribuido de manera decisiva a demostrar la falta de fundamento de los sistemas sociales históricos y la necesidad de reemplazarlos por otros menos arbitrarios. Pero, sobre todas las cosas, a pesar del fracaso de la filosofía en el aspecto positivo, el Occidente no concibe otra manera de fundamentar su praxis social y política. La elaboración de los principios de la sociedad justa se encomienda siempre a la filosofía. Y hoy día, la lucha ideológica, es decir la discusión filosófica sobre la esencia de la sociedad justa, es más intensa y apasionada que en los propios tiempos de la Ilustración.

En nuestra época la discusión se centra en torno de la manera como se puede forjar una sociedad más humana y más justa. Todos los sistemas rivales ofrecen fundamentaciones filosóficas, algunas de las cuales presentan incluso aspectos tomados directamente de la metafísica clásica. El marxismo no es sino una filosofía. Los argumentos en favor de las sociedades en las que existe la libertad individual y el método capitalista de producción esgrimen también argumentos de carácter filosófico, algunos de los cuales provienen directamente de la filosofía racionalista de la Ilustración. Hay algunos políticos occidentales que sostienen que la política no debe fundamentarse en doctrinas filosóficas, sino que debe proceder empíricamente, que la sociedad debe irse reajustando de acuerdo a las circunstancias. Pero esta actitud es tan filosófica como cualquier otra. En primer lugar presupone la crítica de las filosofías que pretenden haber llegado a la concepción de la sociedad ideal. Sólo en caso de que estas filosofías sean falsas tiene sentido el rechazarlas. En segundo lugar presuponen la legitimidad de los fines que ellos mismos proponen. Pues de otra manera carece de sentido la acción política. Si esta legitimidad no se fundamenta racionalmente, aunque sea implícitamente, o bien se regresa a criterios religiosos, o mágicos, o se llega a la conclusión de que todas las metas son equivalentes.

Después de un largo proceso, en el que la filosofía racionalista se ve obligada, debido a la aplicación de sus propios métodos, a reajustar sus concepciones más profundas, el Occidente llega a una situación peculiar. La ciencia, es decir la filosofía que ha logrado encontrar una sistematización segura, sigue progresando y nadie duda de su legitimidad ni de su eficacia. La filosofía en sentido tradicional, ha fracasado en sus intentos de encontrar un sistema (basado en evidencias), de principios para la constitutión de la sociedad justa. Pero en cambio en su labor negativa ha alcanzado resultados definitivos. Y el hombre de Occidente espera siempre que la solución al problema de la sociedad justa sea una solución racional, es decir filosófica. Filosófica en sentido amplio, lo que quiere decir que también la ciencia pueda y debe intervenir—hasta donde sea posible—en la solución del problema.

EL IDEAL DE VIDA RACIONAL Y LA POSIBILIDAD DE FORJAR UNA SOCIEDAD JUSTA

(a) El ideal racionalista del conocimiento y el progreso de los métodos de análisis. Quien conoce *desde adentro* el formidable proceso que conduce a la crisis de la matemática, de la lógica y de la física, que caracteriza la historia del conocimiento racional de los últimos lustros, llega a la conclusión de que dicha crisis se ha debido a un progreso en la vía del conocimiento racional. No puede ya dudarse de que existe un avance seguro de la racionalidad. Y de que el hombre de Occidente, hoy día, de manera aún más definida que en el pasado, cifra el sentido de la historia en la organización de la vida mediante la utilización de los principios aprehendidos por la razón. En consecuencia, la función del intelectual en la vida política de Occidente es hoy día más clara y definida que nunca. El intelectual está constitutivamente relacionado con la praxis política, puesto que la praxis, al igual que toda actividad humana debe encauzarse por medio de principios racionales. Pero el concepto que el occidental tenía de la razón ha sufrido variaciones de detalle. A través de un proceso de profundas repercusiones, el concepto de la razón ha sufrido reajustes, se ha limitado en relación a ciertos principios, pero se ha reforzado en relación a otros. A pesar de ciertas restricciones, el avance que se ha podido realizar en la racionalización cada vez amplia de las diversas regiones del mundo, ha sido espectacular. Todo esto cambia las perspectivas de la razón para la fundamentación de la praxis política. Hasta el momento, debido al desajuste natural entre la teoría y la praxis, la labor ideológica ha estado dominada por concepciones filosóficas anteriores al proceso de reajuste. Es, por eso, urgente, utilizar los nuevos resultados metodológicos en la fundamentación de la praxis política. Se trata de una labor gigantesca, en la que deben intervenir planteamientos filosóficos y científicos de los más diversos alcances.

(b) El principio de la no arbitrariedad *y la racionalidad de la praxis.* El problema fundamental que debe abordar el intelectual en relación a la posibilidad de una praxis racional es el del fracaso de la filosofía clásica en el intento de elaborar un sistema evidente de principios normativos. La crítica filosófica ha mostrado que los sistemas tradicionales no tenían ningún fundamento.

Si se parte de la experiencia histórica de que ha sido imposible a la filosofía elaborar un sistema de principios evidentes para fundamentar la praxis política, se puede hacer una hipótesis que esclarece el panorama de manera inmediata: *no existen principios racionales evidentes que permiten encauzar la praxis humana.* Esta hipótesis tiene la fuerza de que mientras no se encuentre un sistema evidente de principios, no puede demostrarse su falsedad. Y una experiencia histórica milenaria muestra que la probabilidad de encontrar dicho sistema es prácticamente nula.

La hipótesis significa únicamente que no existe una evidencia positiva. Es decir que no es posible mostrar que ciertas acciones son intrínsecamente buenas, mientras que otras son intrínsecamente malas. O sea, la evidencia falla cuando se trata de encontrar criterios de acción concreta, por ejemplo, en relación a valores de nacionalidad, de moralidad sexual, de ética económica, etc. Pero nada dice sobre la posibilidad de encontrar algún criterio negativo de racionalidad. Creemos que este criterio existe.

Si recordamos lo que hemos dicho, vemos que toda actividad racional presenta un aspecto negativo: la *no arbitrariedad*. Lo que más impresiona del conocimiento racional es que su poder de convicción se impone, mediante una fuerza intrínseca, a todas las voluntades individuales. No hay ninguna persona, por más vigor físico o espiritual que tenga, que pueda cambiar los resultados del conocimiento racional. El conocimiento racional tiene sus propias leyes, sus propios principios, y lo fundamental de ellos, no es sólo que son de tal o cual manera, sino que *no pueden ser cambiados por la voluntad de los hombres*. Es posible que a través de algún proceso histórico los hombres lleguen a la conclusión de que ciertos principios no tenían la evidencia que se les atribuyó, mientras que otros sí la tienen. Pero se trata de un proceso puramente racional, es el propio proceso del conocimiento racional el que nos conduce a dicho resultado, no la voluntad de los individuos. Por eso todo principio racional, tiene siempre un aspecto negativo: *es no arbitrario*. La *no arbitrariedad es el principio más general posible de la racionalidad*.

Mientras más se medita sobre el principio de no arbitrariedad, más se capta su carácter esencial. Si la razón humana tiene algún sentido, no puede ser arbitraria, no puede depender de la voluntad individual, no puede variar conforme al capricho de los hombres. La no arbitrariedad es, pues, un principio universal y constitutivo de la vida racional. Y por eso también *se aplica a la esfera de la praxis*. Así como una proposición arbitraria, no puede ser un conocimiento racional, *así, un acto arbitrario de voluntad no puede originar una acción racional*.

Este enunciado coincide con la experiencia histórica. El éxito de la crítica de los sistemas sociales históricos se debe a que demostró que *estos sistemas eran arbitrarios*. Al demostrar que no existía ningún fundamento racional que permitiera justificarlos, demostró que eran arbitrarios, y en consecuencia que no había ningún motivo para conservarlos. Toda la crítica filosófica de los sistemas sociales presupone la evidencia de que la arbitrariedad se opone a la razón.

El error de la filosofía racionalista consistió en tratar de ir más allá de la no arbitrariedad, en buscar afanosamente, un sistema completo de principios que permitiese ajustar la acción humana a normas positivas. Por eso fracasó en su búsqueda, porque de acuerdo a nuestra hipótesis, este sistema no existe. *La racionalidad de la praxis se reduce al principio de la no arbitrariedad*.

(c) El principio de no arbitrariedad y el horizonte de los sistemas equivalentes. Si se acepta que el único principio racional de la praxis es la no arbitrariedad, se ve de inmediato que ello no anula la posibilidad de *construir* sistemas positivos y detalla-

dos que permitan encauzar la acción humana. Una cosa es que no existan evidencias en relación a estos sistemas y otra que sean irracionales. Si el principio de la praxis racional es la no arbitrariedad, entonces todo lo que no sea arbitrario *es racionalmente aceptable.* Si los sistemas sociales históricos fueron criticados y rechazados por la filosofía, ello se debió a que eran arbitrarios. Si no hubieran sido arbitrarios, habría sido imposible demostrar su falta de fundamento.

El único problema que se presenta ante el planteamiento de la tesis es el del rigor. Es la exigencia de rigor la que ha llevado a la filosofía a rechazar los sistemas de encauzamiento de la praxis. En consecuencia todo planteamiento sobre la racionalidad de la praxis, ya sea en su aspecto positivo o negativo exige una semántica precisa. Naturalmente, se trata de un problema difícil. Tratar de encontrar una definición rigurosa de no arbitrariedad nos llevaría muchas páginas. Pero creemos que el problema puede resolverse positivamente. Por el momento hacemos la hipótesis de que se puede. Y nos contentamos con el hecho de que el concepto de *imposición* permite aclarar el concepto de no arbitrariedad. Sin pérdida de generalidad se puede saber cuando la acción de una persona en relación a otra es arbitraria. A procede arbitrariamente en relación a B cuando *le impone* un cauce de acción en contra de su voluntad. El hombre arbitrario es el que decide cómo deben actuar los otros sin tener en cuenta su voluntad. En consecuencia basta que un sistema de principios permita organizar la sociedad de tal manera que ningún individuo pueda *imponer* sus decisiones a los demás, para que sea racionalmente aceptable. Todo sistema de principios (valores éticos, normas jurídicas, etc.) que permita la existencia de una sociedad no arbitraria es racionalmente aceptable.

En principio no existe límite numérico para la existencia de tales sistemas. La situación puede compararse, en cierto sentido, a la de los sistemas matemáticos, abstractos. Lo único que se exige para que se pueda constituir un sistema matemático, es que sea consistente, es decir que no sea contradictorio. Así mismo, lo único que se exige a un sistema social cualquiera para que sea racional, es que sea no arbitrario.

(d) Posibilidad de elaborar un sistema concreto de fundamentación racional de la praxis. Si se adopta como principio positivo que toda persona humana es un fin en sí, se dispone de un postulado que permita organizar la sociedad sobre la base de la no arbitrariedad. Este principio que podemos denominar principio de la *autotelia* es constitutivo del humanismo moderno.

Que toda persona sea un fin en sí, significa que la meta de su existencia es el desarrollo máximo de todas sus posibilidades. El unico límite es el de la no arbitrariedad. Si toda persona tiene el derecho de desarrollar sus posibilidades humanas al máximo, es evidente que ninguna otra tiene el derecho de tomarla como medio para realizar sus propios fines. Porque entonces recorta las posibilidades del que ha sido tomado como instrumento. El hecho de tomar a otro como instrumento, significa que se le imponen cauces arbitrarios. Mientras un hombre es instrumento de otro, tiene que someterse a la voluntad del otro, el otro le impone pautas de comportamiento.

FRANCISCO MIRÓ QUESADA

Partiendo del principio positivo de la *autotelia* se deduce una serie de consecuencias fundamentales que imponen determinado carácter a toda sociedad que pretenda ser racional. Se deduce que para que una sociedad racional o justa no debe permitir ninguna clase de discriminación, no puede ser imperialista, no puede permitir la explotación de unos hombres por otros, y sobre todas las cosas, no puede permitir la constitutión de un poder arbitrario. *El control del poder por la totalidad de la colectividad es una de las consecuencias inescapables del principio de no arbitrariedad.* Vemos así como partiendo del principio de la no arbitrariedad como único principio de la racionalidad práctica se puede constituir una sociedad en la cual se reconocen una serie de rasgos de los ideales, que a través de los siglos, han ido tomando cuerpo en la sociedad occidental. La democracia queda firmemente fundada. *Todo tipo de totalitarismo,* sea cual sea su intención, queda radicalmente excluído. Porque el totalitarismo supone la inexistencia de reglas para controlar el poder. En consecuencia todo gobierno totalitario significa que el grupo gobernante impone sus decisiones de manera arbitraria. Pero asimismo *queda excluída toda justificación de una sociedad en que existan privilegios económicos o sociales.* El resultado parece ser una sociedad que coincide en parte con los ideales históricos, pero que presenta caracteres sui géneris, algunos de los cuales pueden ser desconcertantes.

Aplicando los principios de la lógica moderna, se pueden deducir inagotables consecuencias, es decir principios concretos positivos o negativos de encauzamiento de la acción racional. Se trata de una perspectiva apasionante que hasta el momento no ha sido explorada a fondo. Uno de los aspectos más interesantes es que, algunas actividades pueden quedar rigurosamente reglamentadas, mientras que otras, que en nuestras sociedades occidentales están muy reglamentadas, quedan totalmente indeterminadas.

Desde luego, como en toda construcción de la razón, tienen que presentarse ambiguedades y problemas de difícil si no imposible solución. Habrá siempre casos dudosos, en los que es sumamente difícil saber si una acción es arbitraria o nó. Pero en principio es siempre posible reducir cada vez más los rezagos de arbitrariedad. La sociedad justa se presenta así, como un ideal al cual podemos irnos acercando cada vez más, como se acerca una variable a su límite. El problema fundamental es, desde luego, el del control del poder, o, en términos más técnicos, el de la determinación de las jerarquías. Se trata de un campo de riqueza extraordinaria en el que el intelectual moderno tiene mucho que decir. Nuestro actual sistema democrático, que surge precisamente, como un afán de forjar una sociedad justa, eliminando la arbitrariedad mediante un control del poder, no es sino un primer intento. Es evidente que la tesis de los tres poderes permite dar un paso considerable en la eliminación de la arbitrariedad. Pero no es sino un primer paso. Desde el punto de vista de la eliminación de la arbitrariedad, nuestra democracia está en la infancia. Debido a la simplicidad del esquema es imposible, en las democracias actuales, controlar innumerables factores de arbitrariedad, especialmente en las relaciones económico-políticas. Los filósofos racionalistas descubrieron la verdadera vía. Demolieron los fundamentos de los sistemas sociales basados en el dominio arbitrario de ciertos grupos y trataron de construir un sistema en donde fuera imposible la arbitrariedad. Pero la falta de adecuados medios analíticos, el atraso de las ciencias sociales, la inexperiencia de los primeros pasos, hicieron imposible la construcción de un sistema verdaderamente eficaz.

(e) Los dos niveles de racionalidad en la praxis social. Una vez determinado el punto de partida, la realidad social se organiza a través de un riguroso análisis racional. En efecto, desde un punto de vista estrictamente racional, si se acepta el principio humanista (o cualquier otro), la organización social se concibe como un medio para realizarlo. Se pasa así de un campo puramente principista a un campo instrumental. Y es precisamente en este campo en donde el conocimiento racional ha hecho los mayores progresos. La relación medio-fin es uno de los tipos de relación que puede ser racionalizada de manera más rigurosa. En general dado un fin cualquiera, existen varias maneras de cumplirlo. En análisis racional, consiste en encontrar la manera más eficiente. Desde luego el concepto de eficiencia es relativo, pues se puede tratar de eficiencia en relación al tiempo empleado, a la cantidad de material disponible, al costo de la operación, etc. Pero planteado el tipo de eficiencia que se persigue es con frecuencia posible determinar el *medio optimal* para realizar el fin. La sociedad Occidental, gracias al desarrollo de las disciplinas lógico-matemáticas y a su creciente aplicación a los datos empíricos ha logrado una sistematización creciente de las optimaciones. El cálculo de las optimaciones para la realización de los fines, es el fundamento, en sentido general, de la técnica. Gran parte de la historia de Occidente gira en torno del desarrollo de la técnica. De manera constante y con velocidad creciente, el hombre de Occidente ha ido creando nuevas disciplinas analíticas y ha sido capaz de encontrar optimaciones para la realización de fines cada vez más amplios y complicados. Los modernos procedimientos de la economía matemática y de la cibernética están ampliando las posibilidades de calcular las optimaciones de los medios para los más diversos fines. En algunos casos, pueden calcularse optimaciones que hace apenas unos años ni siquiera tenía sentido plantearse. Esto permite tener la certeza de que los problemas que plantea el ideal de sociedad justa, basado en el principio humanista, pueden ser tratados con posibilidades de éxito cada vez mayor. Todo esto hace posible prever en medida cada vez más amplia y rigurosa los dinamismos sociales, y esta previsión permite planear los desarrollos del conglomerado social hacia metas concretas.

En principio es por eso posible analizar racionalmente los diversos medios que deben emplearse para acercarse cada vez más al ideal de la sociedad justa, es decir, al ideal de una sociedad en que todo ser humano sea considerado como un fin en sí. Desde luego, la problemática presenta una complicación extraordinariamente frondosa. Es necesario resolver problemas económicos, sociológicos, etnológicos, psicológicos, pedagógicos, etc. Pero en principio es posible encontrar optimaciones. Vemos que, en este campo, la ciencia tiene un campo inagotable. El intelectual tiene aquí también, al igual que en el campo filosófico, la oportunidad de contribuir de manera directa a la racionalización de la praxis.

En sentido amplio, se trata de la misma tarea. Ya hemos visto que, desde el punto de vista del ideal de vida racional, no existe diferencia de esencia, entre la ciencia y la filosofía. La ciencia no es sino filosofía rigorizada, filosofía que ha podido encontrar un método seguro para racionalizar cierta región del mundo. Al decir que, de acuerdo con la vigencia de racionalidad de la Cultura Occidental, la filosofía tiene la misión de decir como debe ser la sociedad justa, nos referimos a la totalidad del conocimiento racional. En realidad la racionalización del mundo tiene dos niveles: un nivel puramente principista y un nivel relacional o instrumental. En el nivel principista se determina cuál debe ser la meta suprema de la sociedad justa, cuáles deben ser los principios que guíen la acción de los hombres. En el nivel relacional se determina cuáles son los medios más aptos para cumplir esta meta, para realizar dichos principios. Debido a los inmensos progresos realizados por la ciencia y la técnica occidentales, el nivel relacional en la racionalización de la praxis ha adquirido dimensiones inesperadas.

La determinación de los principios supremos de la acción, de acuerdo con la tradición, se deja a la filosofía. Pero hemos visto, que la exigencia de rigor que se impone a sí mismo todo conocimiento racional, reduce al mínimo el campo de estos principios. La moderna exigencia de rigor, derivada del progreso en los métodos de análisis y de la experiencia del fracaso de los grandes sistemas, nos ha conducido hacia un sólo principio de carácter negativo. Puede decirse que el principio de la no arbitrariedad es el único principio de encauzamiento de la praxis que ha sido determinado por la filosofía en sentido clásico, es decir, en tanto disciplina cognoscitiva aún no suficientemente rigorizada. Una vez hecho esto, se deja todo lo demás a la ciencia. Ya el planteamiento del principio humanista rebasa los marcos de la sistemática clásica en tanto exige un análisis semántico, que puede plantearse de manera científica, o por lo menos muy cercana de la ciencia, mediante los modernos métodos de análisis lingüístico. Vemos, así, que, tanto la ciencia como la filosofía, de acuerdo con las pautas de la Cultura Occidental, tienen la función de determinar los cauces de la praxis. Y esto refuerza al máximo la visión clásica del intelectual, como el hombre que debe determinar los fundamentos de la política. Hoy día la política se funda doblemente en el conocimiento. La filosofía le sirve para determinar los principios generales de la acción, lo que, en relación con la política, significa justificar el sentido de la acción partidaria; y la ciencia para ofrecer las mejores soluciones a los problemas prácticos que plantea la necesidad de realizar los principios proclamados en la ideología. En el mundo actual, en que el Occidente ha ingerido, como una gigantesca ameba a todas las demás culturas, la relación entre el intelectual y la política alcanza su máxima claridad y su más hondo sentido. Después de una dramática crisis en la cual ha sido necesario revisar el significado del conocimiento racional, el viejo ideal de racionalidad ha adquirido aún mayor vigencia. A pesar de todos los fracasos, de todas las frustraciones, a pesar de que fuerzas irracionales casi han logrado destruir la civilización occidental y toda la raza humana, el ideal de una sociedad racional o justa es la gran meta de la historia y el conocimiento racional, la única esperanza de lograrla.

(a) *El compromiso de los intelectuales.* Las consideraciones que anteceden muestran que el hecho de ser intelectual significa un serio compromiso consigo mismo y con la colectividad a la cual se pertenece. Asumir la condición de intelectual, cualquiera que sea el compo que se elija, significa *asumir con plena consciencia* el ideal de vida racional que constituye la vigencia fundamental de Occidente. Las vigencias, en relación a las colectividades son presupuestos no analizados. Se practican de manera "natural," constituyen la "atmósfera" cultural que se respira. Pero ello no quiere decir que un grupo de hombres no tenga conciencia de ellas. Tal vez, la toma de conciencia de ellas, presupone la existencia de otras vigencias, cuya acción espontánea hace posible la toma de conciencia. Pero el hecho innegable es que el ideal de racionalidad es una vigencia de la cultura Occidental y que el intelectual tiene conciencia de ella. Es él quien ha contribuído a perfeccionarla y difundirla, y quien ha sabido mantenerla en momentos de crisis. Por eso al elegir su destino, el intelectual, queriéndolo o sin querer, toma la decisión de dedicar su vida a la realización del ideal de vida racional. El que decide dedicar su vida al conocimiento, decide aceptar los principios que hacen posible el conocimiento. Y el principio supremo del conocimiento es que la verdad no depende del arbitrio individual, sino de ciertas evidencias y reglas que el individuo encuentra en sí mismo. Ser intelectual significa, por eso, sea cual sea el campo de estudio que se haya elegido, estar decidido a no aceptar sino la propia evidencia para la solución de los problemas. En consecuencia *la profesión de intelectual es incompatible con todo tipo de arbitrariedad.* La actitud arbitraria, la prepotencia, es la actitud irracional por excelencia. Y el intelectual, si quiere estar de acuerdo consigo mismo, no puede someterse a ella.

Es cierto que el mundo los conocimientos es tan vasto que un intelectual puede dedicarse a un campo restringido, con total prescindencia de las condiciones políticas imperantes en la colectividad a la que pertenece. Es verdad que así ha sucedido en numerosas ocasiones. Pero ni siquiera este intelectual está seguro de poder decir toda su verdad. Pues es imposible predecir hasta donde es capaz de llegar el análisis racional. Cualquiera que sea el campo, pueden descubrirse verdades que no son del agrado del grupo dominante.

Pero hay ciertos campos en que es imposible dedicarse a la vida intelectual sin producir profundos impactos en la vida colectiva. Hay ciertos aspectos de la filosofía y de la ciencia que constantemente chocan con los intereses de los grupos dominantes. Y es imposible dedicarse a ellos sin despertar las más enconadas resistencias. El intelectual que no tiene la energía suficiente de defender sus puntos de vista contra las presiones de los grupos de interés, es rápidamente silenciado.

De acuerdo con los anteriores análisis, no hay ninguna razón que obligue al intelectual a mantenerse en su posición. Se trata más bien de una cuestión de autenticidad. El intelectual auténtico elige la verdad y la no arbitrariedad y es capaz de luchar hasta las últimas consecuencias para mantener su actitud. El que es incapaz de mantener su actitud, es un intelectual frustrado. Se trata de un carácter intrínseco de la vocación intelectual. Debido a la dinámica natural de las sociedades históricas, la condición de intelectual exige una energía especial para poderse mantener. Existe por eso lo que podría llamarse el *honor intelectual,* es decir *la decisión inconmovible de cumplir hasta el fin el destino elegido.* Es porque han habido intelectuales que han sido capaces de mantener sus puntos de vista, que la filosofía y la ciencia han sido capaces de disolver los prejuicios y las vigencias que permitían a los grupos dominantes perpetuarse en el poder. Es porque han existido intelectuales que han sido capaces de correr todos los riesgos que hoy día se han roto todas las trabas psicológicas que antaño se alzaban en el camino hacia la sociedad justa.

Cuando se habla del intelectual comprometido se piensa generalmente en el compromiso con los movimientos políticos. Pero en realidad el compromiso es mucho más hondo. El hecho de acercarse o no a algún partido político depende del temperamento de cada intelectual y de las circunstancias históricas de su colectividad. Pero actúe o no actúe en la política militante, el intelectual, por el hecho de serlo está ya comprometido: está comprometido a decir la verdad y este compromiso tiene mayores consecuencias y le trae mayores presiones y peligros que cualquier otro. El intelectual es el depositario de los conocimientos racionales acumulados a través de los siglos por la Cultura Occidental, y es el encargado de aumentar el acervo. En tanto los conocimientos verdaderos se oponen a los intereses de los grupos dominantes, *el intelectual está siempre potencialmente en peligro porque es el hombre que el Occidente ha elegido para luchar contra la arbitrariedad.*

(b) El horizonte abierto. Desde que nuestra cultura adquiere sus vigencias definitivas hasta el presente el intelectual ha cumplido su compromiso a través de peripecias sin fin. Venciendo resistencias que parecían insuperables, un grupo creciente de hombres de Occidente, han buscado la verdad y han dicho su palabra. Algunas de las verdades encontradas se han contrapuesto, a través de la historia, a los intereses de los grupos dominantes. Entre los intelectuales y los intereses creados, ha existido, por eso, una tensión permanente. Según las diferentes épocas, la tensión ha sido más o menos fuerte, más o menos explícita. Pero siempre ha existido, y siempre existirá. Es una ley de la historia, que cuando una clase o un grupo ascienden al poder, traten de perpetuarse en él. Y esta tendencia a la permanencia encuentra su mayor obstáculo en la existencia del conocimiento racional. El afán de poder tiende a deformar la visión de la verdad y a utilizar los resultados del conocimiento racional para justificar privilegios. Pero la actitud auténticamente racional, tiende a descubrir y a exponer la verdad con total independencia de los intereses particulares. De allí la tensión, de allí que los grupos conservadores, es decir, los grupos que tienden a perpetuarse en el poder, consideren con frecuencia a los intelectuales como peligrosos izquierdistas, como extremistas que deben ser cuidadosamente alejados de la cosa pública. Este fenómeno es universal. Allí donde hay grupos que proceden arbitrariamente, sea cual sea la doctrina que utilizan para justificar su posición de dominio, allí los intelectuales son incómodos. Se trate de la Francia de Luis XVI, de los estados domina-

dos por la burguesía liberal, del totalitarismo nazi o del totalitarismo comunista, el intelectual es siempre el hombre que proclama verdades que incomodan a los grupos dominantes. El barón de Holbach, vuelve a existir bajo la personalidad de Bertrand Russell, de Sartre, de Camus, de Einstein, de Djilas o de Evtushenko.

La tensión presenta aspectos complicados y a veces impredecibles. Pero a la larga se resuelve en favor del intelectual. Porque el intelectual representa la más prístina vigencia de la sociedad en que vive: el ideal de vida racional que matiza todas las manifestaciones de Occidente. En Occidente las evidencias racionales terminan tarde o temprano por imponerse. Las resistencias vienen de los más diversos grupos e instituciones. Vienen de la aristocracia, de las empresas capitalistas o de los partidos políticos totalitarios. Pero una vez que una verdad echa a correr, no hay nada ni nadie que pueda evitar que los occidentales terminen por creer en ella. Es posible que una dictadura sangrienta pueda impedir su reconocimiento oficial durante largos años. Es posible que una dictadura universal, mediante métodos de terror, pudiese deformar la verdad durante un tiempo indeterminado. Pero la experiencia histórica nos dice lo contrario, la experiencia histórica nos dice que los hombres que se han valido de la razón para llegar a la verdad han logrado disolver todas las falsedades que los grupos dominantes han esgrimido en Occidente para perpetuarse en el poder. Nos dice también que han encontrado formas de organización social que han significado progresos definitivos en la lucha por la eliminación de la arbitrariedad.

A través de una lucha a veces heroica, los intelectuales han avanzado ya un largo trecho en el proceso eliminatorio que constituye una de las glorias de Occidente. Es cierto que hay una enorme porción del mundo en donde se trata de deformar la verdad para ponerla al servicio de los intereses políticos. En algunos lugares, como en países totalitarios, la presión de los grupos dominantes es tan agresiva y brutal como en la Europa de los siglos pasados. En otros, como en ciertos países subdesarrollados y algunos países capitalistas la presión se reduce a la presión económica y a los mecanismos de propaganda. De cuando en cuando una asonada o una revolución relámpago bastan para contener el peligro de las *ideas disolventes de los intelectuales*. Pero en los países más importantes de Occidente, los intelectuales pueden hablar con escaso peligro. Incluso en los países subdesarrollados el peligro es cada vez menor y las ideas renovadoras de la ciencia y de la filosofía tienen cada día mayor acogida en los círculos de todo tipo.

En los países más avanzados puede seguirse con extraordinaria nitidez el grandioso proceso de eliminación de la arbitrariedad que constituye el sentido de la historia occidental. Este proceso ha entrado en una nueva etapa. Debido a los resultados definitivos alcanzados por la crítica filosófica contra los grupos dominantes de los siglos XVII, XVIII y XIX, la etapa del desenmascaramiento ha terminado. No ha terminado como necesidad permanente de luchar contra los argumentos pseudo-filosóficas y pseudo-científicos utilizados por las oligarquías y las cliques totalitarias para afianzarse en el poder. Porque la lucha contra los hombres que utilizan inauténticamente los resultados del conocimiento racional para defender sus intereses no terminará nunca. Mientras la humanidad exista habrán hombres que luchen por la verdad y hombres que traten de utilizar la verdad para defender sus intereses. Pero la etapa del desenmascaramiento ha terminado en el sentido de que *no es necesario disolver más vigencias* para hacer que impere la evidencia del conocimiento racional. El sentido de la filosofía como técnica de desenmascaramiento no es de ninguna manera la discusión filosófica contra grupos que utilizan la filosofía (en el sentido genérico de conocimiento racional de cualquier tipo) para satisfacer afanes de poder. El verdadero sentido del desenmascaramiento es la lucha contra las *vigencias que son utilizadas* (a veces incluso con la mejor buena fe del mundo) *para justificar la situación de privilegio de los grupos que están en el poder.* Si la lucha se hubiera reducido a la mera discusión filosófica habría sido mucho más fácil. Desde que un grupo dominante desciende a la discusión filosófica de igual a igual, está bajando de su pedestal y es vulnerable. Lo significativo de la autojustificación de los grupos dominantes es que en ella se emplean vigencias, que son, a veces, muy fuertes y profundas. Así, en el siglo XVIII, la principal vigencia contra la que lucharon los enciclopedistas fue la creencia—enraizada a través de siglos de intangibilidad—en el derecho divino de los reyes. La filosofía, mediante análisis basados en evidencias racionales que se imponían a todo aquel que se decidía a seguirlos, disolvió esta vigencia. En el siglo XIX, los intelectuales de izquierda disolvieron una vigencia que se basaba en una extrapolación de resultados estrictamente racionales de las ciencias físicas. Los grupos capitalistas justificaban su acción utilizando la vigencia de las leyes naturales de la economía. Se trataba de una vigencia menos profunda y genérica que la anterior. Pero de todas maneras, en relación a los círculos económicos y políticos e incluso académicos, la creencia en las leyes sacrosantas de la economía fue una creencia no analizada durante muchas décadas. Lo mismo puede decirse del nacionalismo que permitía justificar todos los actos de agresión y de imperialismo de los grupos gobernantes, del racismo, etc.

Esta etapa ya ha terminado. Hoy día *el horizonte de Occidente está abierto a la razón.* Prácticamente no hay vigencias que puedan ser utilizadas contra el progreso de la racionalidad. Es cierto que aún existen vigencias muy sólidas al lado de la vigencia de racionalidad. Pero estas vigencias no se oponen ya al ideal de vida racional. Existen aún vigencias nacionales y religiosas. Hoy día es posible, en nombre de los sentimientos patrios crear inmensos movimientos de opinión. Pero nadie se atreve ya a sostener que su país tiene derecho de conquistar a otro para explotarlo a su favor. Asimismo, las vigencias religiosas son aún muy fuertes. Tal vez hasta se note cierto renacimiento de los sentimientos religiosos en Occidente. Pero a nadie se le ocurre que en nombre de la religión debe prohibirse la investigación y la difusión de la verdad. En Occidente no hay ya ninguna vigencia que pueda emplearse con probabilidades de éxito para frenar el proceso de racionalización que caracteriza la marcha de su historia. *Pero esto es lo mismo que decir que no hay ninguna vigencia capaz de frenar el proceso hacia la no arbitrariedad, pues ambos procesos no son sino uno y el mismo.*

(c) La política como técnica social: tarea del intelectual moderno. En el Occidente de nuestros días el ideal de vida racional se expande sin límites y envuelve al universo entero. La meta de la historia es la racionalización total del universo. Los prejuicios desaparecen, los dogmatismos, incluso los del propio pensamiento racional, son superados. El hombre se encuentra libre, con una razón en constante actividad, con una ciencia en constante desarrollo, con una técnica que crece sin término. La razón del hombre moderno se torna prometeica.

Ante este horizonte abierto a la racionalidad, la relación entre el intelectual y la política, dentro de los moldes definitivos que le impone la vigencia constitutiva, se va transformando. Pasa de una labor de crítica y de desenmascaramiento, a una labor de forjación. Las metas se esclarecen hasta la transparencia. El ideal humanista se impone en todos los ámbitos. La meta de la historia es la liberación de todos los hombres para que cada uno de ellos pueda realizar plenamente sus posibilidades humanas. El problema del conocimiento racional ya no es disolver los prejuicios que se oponen a la organización de una sociedad no arbitraria, sino el de encontrar las mejores maneras de organizar los recursos naturales y humanos disponibles para alcanzar la meta de liberación final.

El problema fundamental de la filosofía política es el problema de la optimación. El pensamiento racional se trasforma de técnica de desenmascaramiento en técnica de optimación. *La política se concibe así como una ténica social.* La política consiste en la organización de los recursos naturales y humanos para forjar la sociedad justa, es decir, para forjar una sociedad organizada de tal manera que impida la arbitrariedad en las relaciones humanas.

Debido a la división, ya imposible de evitar (pero de cuya contingencia debemos estar siempre alertas so peligro de desconocer por completo la idea de conocimiento racional) entre la ciencia y la filosofía, la forjación intelectual de la sociedad justa exige una división del trabajo. Los filósofos y los científicos (empleando a la palabra "ciencia" en el sentido genérico que involucra a las ciencias naturales y sociales), tienen ante sí la tarea de determinar el tipo de organización social más adecuado para realizar sobre la Tierra el principio de la no arbitrariedad. Los problemas que aún no pueden ser resueltos mediante métodos rigurosos, pero que, naturalmente, pueden ser tratados de manera racional, es decir de manera que permita un acuerdo cada vez creciente sobre los resultados y una clara conciencia de los puntos no rigorizables (en el estado presente de la cuestión) corresponden a la filosofía.

Los problemas que pueden ser abordados mediante métodos rigurosos, es decir, científicos, se distribuyen entre las diversas ciencias particulares. La política, en tanto racionalización de la praxis humana, puede concebirse, de esta manera como una pirámide, cuya cúspide consta de los principios supremos que deben encauzar la acción humana, y cuya base se asienta sólidamente en la ciencia positiva. Partiendo de la determinación de las metas, que se establecen de acuerdo al principio de la no arbitrariedad, a través de la econometría, la cibernética, la teoría de la información, las diferentes ciencias sociales, las ciencias naturales en tanto permiten el perfeccionamiento de la utilización de los recursos a través de la técnica industrial, el hombre, por medio de su razón, se aboca a la forjación de un mundo nuevo. La política se concibe como la actividad racional para alcanzar esta trasformación del mundo de la manera más rapida y eficaz. El político es el hombre que pretende el poder para poner en marcha la trasformación o para conducirla de manera más eficaz y auténtica. El político se constituye, así, en esta etapa triunfante del ideal de racionalidad, en *técnico social*. Así como las técnicas físicas consisten en trasformar la realidad física para ponerla al servicio del hombre, así la técnica social consiste en trasformar la realidad social para poder realizar el ideal de la sociedad justa. El intelectual es el hombre que hace posible que la política se constituya en técnica social.

(d) La lucha por un humanismo consistente. Teóricamente el horizonte abierto hacia la racionalidad que caracteriza al Occidente moderno, hace posible concebir el proceso que conduce (como una variable a su límite) hacia la sociedad justa como una sistematización progresiva de optimaciones. El proceso, debido a su carácter racional, puede compararse a todos los procesos de racionalización. Una vez fijada la meta humanista, se determinan los mejores métodos de acuerdo con los recursos (materiales y humanos) históricamente disponibles. Los recursos varían de acuerdo con el progreso del movimiento general de racionalización del mundo que constituye la esencia de la cultura Occidental. Los métodos de análisis racional avanzan con velocidad creciente. Estos métodos permiten perfeccionar las técnicas de trasformación de la naturaleza y de la sociedad, y este perfeccionamiento hace posible avanzar con eficacia creciente en la forjación de una sociedad cada vez menos arbitraria.

La tarea positiva del intelectual en la política de Occidente, queda, como hemos visto, claramente fijada. El intelectual es el hombre que ha elegido la vía de la racionalidad. Al avanzar en el conocimiento de la realidad natural y social, avanza en la conquista racional del mundo. Y esta conquista permite humanizarlo, ponerlo a disposición del hombre para que éste pueda realizar cada vez más plenamente sus posibilidades. El intelectual, por el mero hecho de serlo, por el mero hecho de dedicarse a racionalizar las diversas regiones de la realidad, ofrece al político el instrumento de trasformación que necesita para avanzar hacia la sociedad justa. Se establece así una proporción directa entre el conocimiento y la sociedad justa. Conforme el conocimiento avanza en la racionalización del mundo, el político va disponiendo de métodos de optimación cada vez más perfectos para trasformar la realidad y de conceptos cada vez más claros para expresar las ideologías y los programas que significan la proclamación del principio humanista.

Pero en este avance sin límites de la racionalidad, en que el intelectual y el político marchan unidos por una misma tarea surgen graves dificultades. Una de ellas es puramente práctica, pero no por eso menos peligrosa. La otra se deriva de la propia vigencia del ideal de vida racional.

Una vez proclamada la meta de la sociedad justa y eliminadas todas las vigencias que se oponían a su universal aceptación, el camino hacia la trasformación social queda claramente trazado. Pero, como es natural, existen fuerzas que se oponen a la trasformación. Tanto la índole humana como el carácter de los diversos dinamismos sociales que constituyen la marcha de la historia, contribuyen a crear *grupos de poder* cuyos intereses se oponen a las trasformaciones exigidas por el ideal humanista. En ciertos países, especialmente en los subdesarrollados, estos grupos tienen una fuerza de alarmantes dimensiones. Debido a procesos que sería demasiado largo analizar, estos grupos concentran la casi totalidad de la riqueza de la nación, poseen el poder político, el poder social, y son capaces de mover todos los hilos necesarios para evitar cualquier trasformación que ponga en peligro sus intereses. El poder que poseen les permite realizar actos de *prepotencia,* es decir actos mediante los cuales imponen su voluntad de manera arbitraria.

Este estado de cosas produce graves tensiones. Porque, debido a la disolución de las viejas vigencias sobre las que los grupos de poder basaban su poderío, no hay nada, absolutamente nada, que impida al pueblo comprender las ideas de trasformación que acompañan a todo planteamiento humanista. En consecuencia, si la situación se prolonga, los grupos de poder corren el riesgo de ser arrollados por una ola de violencia.

Es especialmente interesante observar la situación en algunos países latinoamericanos. Debido a la libertad de prensa y de los medios de propaganda que existe en ellos, en estos últimos tiempos las ideas humanistas de trasformación se han hecho irresistibles. A pesar de que los grupos de prepotencia dominan la mayoría de los medios de expresión, la sola posibilidad de expresión libre ha permitido una veloz difusión de estas ideas, y en las elecciones populares los grupos renovadores han comenzado a triunfar de manera avasalladora. Pero debido a su enorme poder y a la propia naturaleza de los regímenes democráticos, las oligarquías a pesar de la derrota, han logrado conservar el dominio de sutiles mecanismos a través de los cuales influyen en las decisiones políticas. Y esto entorpece de manera, a veces exasperante, el proceso de trasformación hacia la sociedad justa. La amenaza de la violencia se cierne sobre el horizonte de racionalidad que impera ya en estos países.

Lo grave de la violencia es que, por definición, es estrictamente irracional. Toda violencia supone la existencia de la arbitrariedad, incluso cuando se emplea para evitar la arbitrariedad. Si la violencia antiarbitraria se redujera a encarcelar al criminal que atenta contra la vida de los ciudadanos, la situación sería muy simple. Pero la violencia significa la instauración de un régimen dictatorial para evitar que los grupos de poder entorpezcan el proceso de trasformación. Y la dictadura, por esencia, produce situaciones en que un pequeño grupo de hombres impone sus puntos de vista a todos los demás sin que los demás tengan la oportunidad de hacer cambiar las decisiones. Toda dictadura, teóricamente, significa la posibilidad de la arbitrariedad. Y la experiencia histórica nos enseña que toda revolución violenta, por más justa que haya sido su motivación, ha producido situaciones de pavorosa arbitrariedad.

El problema asume visos de verdadera paradoja. El ideal de no arbitrariedad impone la trasformación de la sociedad. Pero esta trasformación no puede hacerse sin

FRANCISCO MIRÓ QUESADA

violencia. Y la violencia, es por definición, la actitud arbitraria. O sea, que para luchar contra la arbitrariedad, hay que emplear la arbitrariedad. O, lo que es lo mismo, para realizar la sociedad justa, hay que valerse de la injusticia.

Si el problema fuera teórico, la paradoja sería insoluble, y el ideal de racionalidad estaría herido de muerte. Pero, como hemos dicho, se trata de un problema puramente práctico. Teóricamente no hay ninguna traba a la organización de una sociedad que evite la arbitrariedad y que reduzca la violencia a los casos en que es necesario impedir que una persona ejerza violencia sobre otra. Pero en la práctica, el poderío de los grupos de dominio genera la posibilidad de someter a toda la colectividad a etapas de violencia de duración indeterminada.

Contra esta posibilidad sólo hay dos maneras de luchar. La primera es intensificar hasta los límites del heroismo la lucha ideológica. Debido a que todas las masas del mundo están hoy ganadas por el ideal de racionalidad, una difusión adecuada de los ideales humanistas contribuye a crear movimientos políticos tan avasalladores que no hay grupo de poder que los pueda resistir. Ya lo hemos visto. En los pueblos de América Latina salvo algunas excepciones las masas votan por quienes representan el ideal humanista y la exigencia de una sociedad justa. Sólo la maniobra política ha permitido a los grupos de poder, ya vacilantes, conservar parte de su fuerza. Todo hace pensar por eso que, en un futuro cercano, los últimos baluartes de la vieja arbitrariedad oligárquica, serán barridos definitivamente. Entonces el proceso humanista hacia la sociedad justa, podrá desarrollarse *de manera consistente,* es decir, sin violencia, dentro de un adecuado sistema democrático.

Pero en el caso trágico de que no pudiera darse pronto este último paso, y la violencia llegara a desatarse, la única actitud consistente con el ideal de vida racional, es considerarla como un desgarramiento, como una limitación de la razón que ha sido rebasada por la realidad. Y aquí el coraje que tantas veces ha exigido la historia del intelectual, alcanzará sus más altas expresiones. Porque la labor del intelectual será la de predicar la necesidad de volver a la razón, la exigencia inflexible de seguir con la trasformación, pero dentro de la libertad y la no arbitrariedad. Su misión será la de—corriendo riesgos a veces mayores que cuando luchaba contra las fuerzas reaccionarias—reducir al mínimo la trágica etapa irracional que ha sido inevitable para hacer posible el advenimiento de la sociedad racional.

Y aquí se presenta el segundo peligro, el peligro derivado de la propia vigencia de la racionalidad. Porque aunque la propia exigencia de rigor que caracteriza al ideal de conocimiento racional ha conducido a los pensadores de Occidente a asumir posiciones filosóficas mucho más prudentes que en el pasado, todavía la vieja tradición especulativa pasa fuertemente en el campo de las ideologías. El propio dinamismo de la razón, mediante las sucesivas depuraciones realizadas a través de las crisis, ha conducido a la filosofía a buscar una fundamentación ideológica que esté de acuerdo con el rigor que exige el ideal del conocimiento racional. Por este motivo la única manera de encontrar una ideología que responda al espíritu moderno de rigor es, como hemos visto, prescindir de los viejos sistemas cuya vaguedad no permite disponer de criterios eficientes de decisión en relación a los problemas que plantea la realización de la sociedad justa. Esto no significa de ninguna manera negar autenticidad filosófica a la metafísica. Significa únicamente ajustarse a la exigencia de rigor que la actual etapa del proceso de racionalización del mundo impone al pensamiento filosófico. La metafísica puede constituir un intento interesante, incluso fundamental, de racionalización de las regiones más profundas de la realidad. Pero no puede constituir de ninguna manera el fundamento filosófico de la praxis política. Por la sencilla razón de que no permite llegar a conclusiones cuya evidencia se imponga universalmente. No permite tampoco ejercer un control sobre las consecuencias de los principios ni sobre la manera como la trasformación de la realidad coincide o no coincide con estas consecuencias. La vaguedad de los sistemas metafísicos tradicionales permite justificar todas las arbitrariedades y no hay manera de demostrar lo contrario. La única salida posible es rechazar todos los planteamientos que no respondan a las exigencias de rigor impuestas por la moderna metodología.

Pero los sistemas filosóficos de viejo cuño, debido al hecho de que en su intención son racionales, a la tradición cultural de Occidente y al poder de sugestión de los líderes políticos, ejercen aún enorme atractivo sobre ciertos sectores ciudadanos. Y algunos sistemas, como el marxismo, y en general todos aquellos que tienen relación con la dialéctica de Hegel, justifican racionalmente la violencia. Para las metafísicas dialécticas, la violencia es una necesidad racional, es una condición necesaria para poder imponer la sociedad justa sobre la tierra. O sea que, este tipo de fundamentación, permite, en apariencia, justificar la violencia y las dictaduras de "duración indeterminada."

En el campo puramente teórico no existe ya ningún peligro de que las filosofías que consideran racional a la violencia puedan ganar la batalla ideológica. La exigencia de rigor del pensamiento moderno es demasiado grande para que la filosofía actual considere válida una tesis que es, lógicamente, una contradictio in adjecto. Además, los modernos métodos de análisis han mostrado hasta la sociedad la total infecundidad de los métodos dialécticos en el sentido hegeliano-marxista. Los mismos marxistas tratan hoy día de modernizar sus puntos de vista y ponerlos a tono con los resultados de la lógica y de la epistemología. Pero en el campo político las tesis que justifican dialécticamente la violencia siguen teniendo atractivo. Es, por eso, de gran importancia que los pensadores que se ocupan de cuestiones ideológicas se esmeren en difundir los resultados de la moderna filosofía sobre la ineficiencia de la dialéctica y en hacer ver que el humanismo consistente, es decir la organización de una sociedad sin violencia, es la única manera de realizar el ideal de vida racional que impulsa el movimineto de trasformación.

Quedan así perfiladas las tareas que el intelectual moderno, en tanto es el hombre llamado a elaborar el fundamento ideológico de la praxis política, debe realizar para contribuir al advenimiento de la sociedad justa. De un lado tiene ante sí una inmensa tarea positiva. Una formidable tarea de forjación, de construcción teórica de una organización social que impida la arbitrariedad. Para hacer esta elaboración—que ya está en marcha—tiene que utilizar todos los recursos de la ciencia y de la filosofía dentro de los marcos de rigor que hoy hacen posible llegar a resultados universalmente válidos. Es la tarea más difícil desde el punto de vista del esfuerzo intelectual. Es una tarea que exige fuerza creadora, ingenio metodológico y amplio dominio en las respectivas especialidades. Es una tarea de racionalización progresiva, de reajustes cada vez más ceñidos al rigor y a la eficacia y que envuelve en sus afanes a la totalidad del universo.

Del otro lado tiene una tarea negativa. Una tarea de vigilancia y de depuración. Debe esforzarse en evitar la violencia, debe preparar el camino para que puedan realizarse trasformaciones cada vez más decisivas en la marcha hacia la sociedad justa sin que sea necesario apelar a la arbitrariedad. Debe hacer esfuerzos ilimitados para dar al dinamismo que constituye el sentido de la historia la consistencia necesaria para evitar que la historia pierda sentido. Ambas tareas son gigantescas y exigen una energía titánica. Sólo una pasión muy honda es capaz de proporcionar la energía necesaria para llevar a cabo una hazaña tan arriesgada. Una pasión que permita correr todos los riesgos. Porque el intelectual debe colocarse necesariamente entre dos fuegos. De un lado, al destruir las vigencias arcaicas, prepara el camino de la revolución; y del otro, al perseguir un humanismo consistente, tiene que oponerse a los brotes de violencia que acompaña a las revoluciones. Y nada hay más peligroso que la soledad de la guerra en todas la sfrentes. Pero el intelectual tiene esta pasión. Porque no debemos olvidar que todo intelectual, por esencia, es un humanista. Y el humanismo, como hemos visto, no es una teoría, es una pasión. Es una pasión que—paradójicamente—sólo puede satisfacerse plenamente por medio de la razón. El intelectual es el más radical de los apasionados porque su pasión es la razón y la razón es la más radical de las afirmaciones humanas. Ser intelectual, afanarse por la racionalización del mundo y afirmar apasionadamente la dignidad de la condición humana es una sola y misma cosa. Ser intelectual es lo mismo que luchar hasta las últimas consecuencias por la liberación de todos los hombres.

THE AMBIGUITIES SUGGESTED BY THE TITLE OF THE CONFERENCE ARE ILLUS-
trated by an innocent mistake in the University newspaper *The Daily Texan;*
for there it has been declared that the subject of our discussion is the role of
the intelligentsia in politics. That is not the title, and as far as I am concerned, it is

not the subject I shall treat here. But it is significant that "intellectuals" and "intelli-gentsia" are thus taken as equivalent. It is, perhaps, as well to begin with a discussion of what I take the word "intelligentsia" to mean, and to explain why it is not applicable to Great Britain. The word is, of course, Russian in origin, and if we look at what it meant in the Russia of the Tsars, we may get some idea of what it means in other countries today, and what it does *not* mean, and never has meant, in Britain.

The Russian intelligentsia were those members of Russian society who had received a fairly serious education, especially an education which opened to them the Western culture which Russia was, slowly and formally, trying to acquire. Most Russians were not literate in Russian; therefore literacy was itself a special mark of distinction. But literacy in Russian or even in Old Slavonic, the literacy of priests and monks, was not enough to qualify one to be a member of the intelligentsia. An "intelligent" was someone who could read French or German or, more rarely, English; someone who had been to the high schools or universities that the Tsars had imposed on the country as part of the westernizing policy of the "great reformer" Peter the Great. But the "intelligent" was, as a rule, disaffected. He was not grateful to the Tsardom for the opportunities it gave him; he was resentful of the opportunities it denied him. More than that, he was resentful of the backwardness of Russia and blamed the autocracy for the humiliating contrast between Russia and Germany and, still more, between Russia and France or Britain. The Russian intelligentsia hankered for a degree of spiritual and intellectual knowledge that they found hard to get inside Russia. It is not accidental that so many of the leaders of the intelligentsia spent a great part of their lives abroad, or that a visit to "Europe" was an opening of doors, an access to wisdom and enlightenment that, it was thought, could not be got at home.

The famous passage of Herzen's *Memoirs* in which he describes his emotions upon arriving in Paris, full of the memories of the Great Revolution, of Camille Desmoulins plucking the green leaves in the Palais Royal garden as the badge of the attackers of the Bastille, is an example of the aspirations and frustrations of the Russian intelligentsia. But Herzen was a very rich man who could afford to live outside Russia and to keep in touch with the West. The poor Russian, often the son of a serf or of a priest, who could not leave Russia and who found the atmosphere of the Tsars' Russia stifling, had no such consolations. So he turned to opposition and to revolution, and in a country as backward economically as nineteenth-century Russia, the openings for these poor members of the educated classes were limited and the pursuit of learning and the use of learning a lone and frustrating career. Trofimov, the "perpetual student" in *The Cherry Orchard,* was typical of many Russians. Not all of them dwelt in the ambience of "good" society or found, like Dr. Chekhov, a serf's son, an opportunity of service. Thousands of them were alienated, unemployed, and driven by good and bad emotions to revolution, like the sons of the chief school inspector Ulianov. Lenin, eminently a member of the intelligentsia, was not as deprived as many were, but the alienation of Lenin and his elder brother from the religious and political piety of their family was symptomatic.

It is possible that a new intelligentsia is growing up in the Soviet Union, alienated from the Soviet establishment and hungering after the intellectual richness of the West. But even if the Russian intelligentsia has had its day, its equivalents are to be found in India, Africa, and all over Latin America. "Perpetual students" are numerous in all these countries. Students are, almost by definition, active in politics, and usually in revolutionary politics. The revolution may be one of the Right as well as of the Left. Goebbels was a perpetual student of the Right, Hitler a spoiled painter. And certainly the existence of tens of thousands of students ready for rioting more serious than any Berkeley knows is a feature of political life in Baghdad, Calcutta, Bogotá, and, now, Spain.

There is not—there never has been—such a class in Britain, certainly not in England and almost certainly not in much poorer Scotland. There have been perpetual students made angry and bitter by their personal misfortunes, deserved or undeserved, like George Gissing and James Thomson, but their discontents have taken the form of such books as *New Grub Street* and of poems like "The City of Dreadful Night." They have not taken the form of revolution or of a total alienation from their native societies.

But if there has been no equivalent of the intelligentsia in Britain, there long has been—and is—an equivalent of the "intellectuals." Again, it is probably desirable to note the origins of the term "intellectual." It came into current use at the time of the Dreyfus case in France, around 1900. The *intellectuels* were the people who defended Dreyfus not only on moral but on intellectual grounds. Scientists, historians, philosophers—they were supposed, on the one hand to be above the mere party battle and, on the other, to be capable, because of their training, of distinguishing the true from the false without being blinded by political or religious passion. The word soon got general currency and has now passed into universal use. We now know, of course, that it was an illusion to suppose that learned men, even, or especially, men learned in the natural sciences, are free from passion or transfer from their laboratories and libraries a spirit of scholarship, that they learned there a practice different from the bitter battlefields of political controversy. It was easy, around 1900, to assume that only men on the Right would blind themselves to evident truths like the innocence of Dreyfus or consciously assert that mere truth did not matter in the face of great national interests. But we now know that men of the Left can be just as passionate and just as credulous. If Léon Blum was shocked and distressed to find that his literary idol Maurice Barrès refused to look at the evidence for the innocence of Dreyfus because he wished and *needed* Dreyfus to be guilty for his own political passions, we have the same story, a generation later, when Romain Rolland refused to learn from Eugene Lyons the truth about the Soviet Union; and Romain Rolland, as a young man, had been one of those most convinced of the moral virtues and total devotion to truth of the *intellectuels*. And the acceptance of the Lysenko nonsense

SIR DENIS BROGAN

by eminent French academics was just as much an insult to the tradition of scholarship and science as any of the credulity displayed in the Dreyfus case by the forces of the Church, the Army, and the State. And if it is true, as I believe it to be, that the most effective defense of Dreyfus was made by Jean Jaurès, it is perhaps worth noting that one of the most mendacious of modern newspapers, *Humanité*, bears on its masthead the formally correct description, "Founded by Jean Jaurès."

Just as we have no intelligentsia, we have no *intellectuels* in this sense in Britain. We have been congratulated on this fact by one of the most acute and learned commentators on modern politics, Raymond Aron, who wrote in 1955, "Great Britain is probably the western country which has dealt with its intellectuals in the most sensible way. As D. W. Brogan once said, 'We British don't take our intellectuals so seriously.' "

But this is not to say that intellectuals as individuals and in various organized forms have not played an important part in British political life for a long time. To go back to the seventeenth century, there were the great wars of pamphlets—pamphlets by Milton, by Harrington, by Filmer, by Locke. All of these pamphleteers were men of erudition—men who had gained some of their prestige from their erudition —and they were more than mere public relations men for interest groups. They were inspirers and, in some ways, creators of interest groups. Locke, as Peter Laslett has shown, was not a mere front man for the Whig oligarchy and, as he has also shown, Sir Robert Filmer was not a mere reactionary pedant but a political thinker with something important to say. Yet these political thinkers were not taken very seriously by the rulers of Church and State. It was an important political thinker in Scotland, Fletcher of Saltoun, who quoted an anonymous and "wise" friend to the effect that it mattered not who "made the laws as long as I can make the ballads." This was a truth, but a half truth. The best ballads were for the Stewarts, but it was the prose of Locke that won the day and the House of Hanover that kept the throne!

It was, I think, in the eighteenth century that something like a group of "intellectuals" could first be identified. By this I do not mean the political pamphleteers paid by the government or by the opposition, of whom the most famous was Dr. Samuel Johnson, who hated the Whigs and Americans almost equally. The beginning of a group that we can call "intellectuals" can be noticed when questions of political economy began to be more important than disputes about "political" religion. Sir William Petty, in the seventeenth century, who invented the term "political arithmetic," was one of the founders of this school of intellectuals. Another was the great skeptical philosopher David Hume. But the most important was Hume's great friend and executor Professor Adam Smith. Indeed, it is one of the odd coincidences of history that two great intellectuals published their most famous contributions to political theory in the same year; for 1776 saw the writing of the Declaration of Independence by Thomas Jefferson (an intellectual if ever there was one) and the publication of *The Wealth of Nations* by Adam Smith. Each had his pupils. I am, however, concerned only with the British pupils of Adam Smith. Among these was Lord Shelburne, descendant of Sir William Petty. Another was the young Prime Minister William Pitt. Adam Smith was the founder of a school whose disciples are still powerful and who, for a long time, provided a political doctrine for most of the rulers of Britain. And, again an odd coincidence, it was in 1776 that the young Jeremy Bentham published his first important political tract, and the combination of Adam Smith's economics and Bentham's moral and political philosophy created the orthodoxy of British political life that lasted well into this century. Of course there were some who reacted against the new orthodoxy. In some ways, Edmund Burke was a disciple of Adam Smith, whom he both read and knew. But the Scot was too rational for the Irishman, and the French Revolution brought out in practice Burke's fundamental skepticism about the unlimited use of reason. In his famous rhetorical passage in *Reflections on the Revolution in France*, Burke deplored the fact that "the age of calculators" had come. He also deplored that the age of "economists" and "Sophisters" had come and that the "Age of Chivalry" was over.

It seems to me that since that time, intellectual schools in Britain and politicians, businessmen, and administrators have oscillated between following Burke and following Smith and Bentham. On the whole, they have talked of Burke and followed Smith and Bentham, but I would not deny that Burke was an intellectual in politics, even if his politics consisted in cutting down to size the role of intellect in politics! The American and French revolutions made the role of the intellectuals far more important and far more dangerous in all countries than it had been in the century preceding these two great events, and it was out of the quarrels and the alarms of the French Revolution that one of the most characteristic instruments of the intellectual in politics was born. For in 1802, the *Edinburgh Review* was founded. With it, an identifiable group of educated men, with a common political bias, tried to appeal to an educated public whom they wished to convert to their faith or, in some instances, to restore the faith of waverers. The polemical magazine was the beginning of the organized intellectuals as a force in British politics. There had been, of course, important political pamphlets ranging from Junius to Burke, and in the *Federalist* the infant United States had produced perhaps the most famous series of pamphlets designed to promote a cause. But the *Edinburgh Review* was an institution which the *Federalist* was not.

After the *Edinburgh Review*, and in answer to it, came the high Tory *Quarterly Review* and the utilitarian *Westminster Review*, as well as a number of magazines designed to defend various branches of the Christian religion. And the contributors to these reviews were in general known and were often persons of considerable political importance. Such were Brougham, Jeffrey, and Macaulay of the *Edinburgh Review*, the most famous and the most effective of these periodicals. But the two Mills, James and John Stuart, were very important bureaucrats indeed in the India Office when Britain really ruled India; and the *Quarterly* and later the *Saturday Review* drew on the services of important Tory politicians as well as on mere intellectuals or men of letters. At the same time, the case for an intellectual class was being stated eloquently and persuasively but in a sense irrelevantly by Coleridge in his plea for a "clerisy." The "clerisy" was to be a kind of intellectual priesthood, the preserver and propagator of the most important intellectual and moral values. It was an idea taken up, held, and imitated by many political parties and many political leaders later. True, Coleridge's "clerisy" was an irrelevant idea in the England in which he launched it, since he tied it to a largely moribund Church of England. But how many "clerisies" have we seen since then! Although Coleridge is not responsible for this, the "ideologist," to borrow a term from Communist practice, is a familiar and formidable figure today. The term "ideologue," a contemptuous description of a theorist in France, is a word we owe to that master of language, Napoleon. He meant it as a term of contempt. But although he was very much an intellectual in France, he did not like, in that role, any rivals.

The real "clerisy" of the age was, of course, that of the Utilitarians who, as writers —even if sometimes unreadable writers like Bentham (he was fortunately a rich man and did not depend on royalties), administrators like the two Mills, legal theorists like Austin, economists like Francis Place and M'Culloch—set out to convert the English people (the Scots were largely converted already) to their rational view of political life. And it is of special interest to note that Utilitarianism is still the basic political "religion" of all successful men in England, although it has been "refuted" by acute thinkers repeatedly since those early days.

It should be observed that the people I have been describing as intellectuals in politics were, almost without exception (Place is one), men who had received expensive educations, then much rarer in Britain than today and very much rarer than in the United States. The Scottish universities, above all Glasgow and Edinburgh, had been great teachers not only of the English but of Europe. Did not Jean-Baptiste Say go on pilgrimage to Glasgow to see the classroom in which Adam Smith had lectured? And if Oxford and Cambridge were very much behind their Scottish sisters, they began to revive in the first half of the nineteenth century, and from that time on the Scottish universities, Oxford, and Cambridge, and University College, London (Bentham's foundation that produced John Stuart Mill and Bagehot), had as one of their main duties the education of a' ruling group with intelligent theories of politics and a readiness to apply them. Perhaps the most important result of this "concern" (as the Quakers put it) for the application of learning to political affairs was the reform, first of all, of the Indian Civil Service by Macaulay and his brother-in-law Charles Trevelyan and then of the Home Civil Service by Gladstone and Northcote. It was Macaulay's simple theory that the higher ranks in the Civil Service should be held by persons who had received extremely arduous intellectual training in the universities. It is true not only because they would presumably be intelligent but because the kind of hard work required at this stage in life to get a man a first in Oxford or Cambridge meant that he had moral virtues and could resist the more familiar temptations of his age! It did not matter very much what the candidates studied or what they were examined in. Any severe test would do. Macaulay, in a humorous fashion, suggested that Cherokee would do. (I have recently discovered from a learned review that the study of Cherokee would indeed be extremely valuable for anybody trying to master linguistics and to get outside the categories of our Indo-European languages. Macaulay, however, did not know this!) He was not a naïve believer in the higher education or even in academic industry. He is supposed to have said of the old Indian Civil Service that its members had been "educated above their ability." But his view was adopted, and from roughly 1870 (and to an impressive degree) the higher Civil Service, an increasingly powerful body, was recruited from people who were by training if not by taste "intellectuals." And it should also be noticed that the great improvement in the academic standards of Oxford and Cambridge, as well as of the Scottish universities, was reflected in the education of the politicians. Peel and Gladstone both got "double firsts" (in classics and mathematics) at Oxford. A good many more leading politicians had had distinguished academic careers, and many persons who had had such careers chose politics—as did H. H. Asquith—when they could equally well have chosen the Civil Service. There was thus a bond of a common education between the ruling class and the governing class, to use and amend William Allen White's distinction. Even if the politicians as a rule had not done as well at the university as the civil servants, they had a common background.

The universities were changing more than their standards. It was an important matter when German philosophy began to be taught in Glasgow and Oxford by Caird and T. H. Green. It was an important matter when Utilitarianism was attacked in Cambridge by the younger Grote, although it was still ably defended by Henry Sidgwick. "Winds of doctrine" were now swirling round even Oxford, and this was reflected in the great newspapers as well as in the great reviews. The Lord Robert Cecil who was one of the chief stars of the conservative *Saturday Review* was to be three times Prime Minister as Marquess of Salisbury. John Morley and James Bryce owed their start in political careers largely to their journalistic competence, and men of this type were to be found in the great political clubs of London, such as the Reform and the Carleton, as well as in the special club of the intellectual class, the Athenaeum.

One result of the change in the teaching of philosophy and economics in the universities was the justification of an abandonment of the strict utilitarian doctrine. T. H. Green was not a very acute or consistent philosopher but he did find philosophical reasons for breaking away from the austere *laissez-faire* policies of the first part of the century. Even John Stuart Mill abandoned these policies, although he tried to save his father's principles at the cost of philosophical confusion. Whether such teachers as Green really influenced policy is open to question. Perhaps the pupils who were to be important politicians—like Alfred Milner—would have come out for extension of state authority even if they had not been provided with philosophical reasons for doing so. But the reasons *were* being provided, and while Herbert Spencer was being nearly deified in America by such businessmen as Andrew Carnegie, his philosophical position was being undermined at home by more respectful attacks than that provided by Carlyle, who called him "the most unending ass in Christendom." The stage was

SIR DENIS BROGAN

set for a new development of the role of the intellectual in British politics. The age of Fabianism was about to begin. By 1880, a new, formally integrated English ruling class was apparent. This was what was later to be called the "Establishment." It would be absurd to pretend that this was mainly composed of intellectuals in any sense of the term. The heirs of great Whig families, like Lord Hartington, had no need to be intellectuals to be important in politics. It sufficed to be the heir to the dukedom of Devonshire. Rich businessmen were going into politics—like W. H. Smith and Joseph Chamberlain. Joe Chamberlain could have been an intellectual had his lot been cast in a slightly different class, but, except toward the end of his life, he did not suffer from the fact that he neither was nor looked like one. W. H. Smith could not have been an intellectual in any time or place or class, but he had solid political talents. Nevertheless, there was, despite bitter party quarrels, a common attitude that marked the professions, literature, science, the arts, and even the law. "Old Father Antic the law" had, in fact, been greatly reformed in practice, if not in doctrine, by the influence of the Benthamites. By this time, the old abuses attacked by Jeremy Bentham and, equally effectively, by Charles Dickens were to be found only in the United States. If there were no deep juristic ideas behind Utilitarian reforms, there was plenty of practical good sense, even in the criminal law, although there were curious reversions like the Labouchere amendment which had, for its most famous result, the conviction of Oscar Wilde.

But the Fabian Society was both a molder of a new England and an aspect of it. It was an organized body of intellectuals, not united by party allegiance or by contributions toward an identifiable party organ like the *Fortnightly* or to a common professional point of view. The Fabian Society included such unsuccessful novelists as the young Bernard Shaw, minor Civil Servants like Sydney Webb, beautiful young society women like Beatrice Potter, future colonial governors, judges, members of Parliament, leading newspapermen, and some divines. Intellectually, the most important early Fabian was Philip Wicksteed, who was a leading Congregational minister, one of the greatest English authorities on Dante, and an extremely clever economist who refuted Marx to the satisfaction of the young Sydney Webb. It was only much later that the salutary effect of Wicksteed's analysis of Marxian theory wore off! The Fabian Society was what H. G. Wells was later to call "the open conspiracy," and demanded no profession of either faith or party allegiance. Men and women of all parties could and did belong to it, but all the Fabians were in favor of extending state action and were convinced that *laissez-faire* was an outmoded doctrine. It was a holding company of all reformist ideas in virtually all fields of public policy. (Since, in modern America, the Fabian Society is regarded by many, especially by Catholics, as almost as dangerous as the Communist Party, it is perhaps worth pointing out that one of its ancestors was Rosmini, a great Italian Catholic philospher who founded the Order of Charity.) The Society eschewed revolutionary tactics. Its rather dull chosen hero was Fabius Cunctator, the Roman dictator who saved the Roman Republic from Hannibal. "Cunctando restituit rem," by delay saving the state. It "bored from within" in a great many bodies ranging from the new London County Council to the Liberal Party and, to some degree, even to the Conservative Party. Its first child was the London School of Economics, and its next that characteristic organ of left-wing intellectuals the *New Statesman*. That a society with so few members, with such comparatively small financial resources, and with such little power of public appeal should yet have been so influential is significant of the importance now attached to the intellectual in politics. I say "influence," not "power," for the importance of the Fabian Society, and especially of the Webbs, in actual political life has been greatly overestimated. But if the importance of the Fabians *is* so overestimated, this is significant of the new respect for the intellectual.

Then the old establishment was being reinforced or attacked by a new generation of intellectuals, of whom the most representative figure was H. G. Wells. He was a graduate not of Oxford or Cambridge or University College, London, but of what was to be the Imperial College of Science. His early novels are admirable documents describing the ambitious young men, often of lower middle-class or upper working-class origins, who were working their way through college or fighting their way into the Establishment and who resented both the pretensions and the stuffiness of the old intellectual order. *Love and Mr. Lewisham* is a document of the first order for the rise of this important subclass and the prophetic fable *The Food of the Gods*, with its discussion of the scientists' admiration for Imperial Germany because it respected the natural sciences, is equally important. The "intellectuals" were, of course, not united. They had had, in a minor way, their Dreyfus Case in the bitter disputes over the policy and morality of the Boer War. Characteristically—and prophetically—the Webbs were in favor of the destruction of the Boer Republics by a more advanced economic society. But many of the Fabians and masses of the liberals—and Liberals—were hostile to the new imperialism, and one of the most important political tracts of this time was J. A. Hobson's *Imperialism*, which influenced Lenin.

By 1914, after eight years of the most brilliant government Great Britain has had for a century, a great many Fabian ideas had been put into legislative form. The Webbs talked to, and to some degree influenced, brilliant young cabinet ministers like Winston Churchill. On the edge of the Cabinet were such brilliant young men of high academic standing as Charles Masterman and Herbert Samuel. In the Cabinet was one of the greatest of British administrators, Lord Haldane, who as Secretary for War had said he wanted a "Hegelian army." Whether he got a Hegelian army or not, he got an army much better prepared for war in 1914 than the British army was in 1939.

But far more important than this success of the intellectuals in politics was the impact of the First World War. For one thing, it called on the services of many intellectuals like the young John Maynard Keynes of the Treasury; for another, it automatically extended the functions of the state and the demand for people able to serve the new, expanding purposes of the state. More or less incidentally, it ruined the old Liberal Party, gave the small Labor Party its chance to become the Opposition and then the Government, and provided the occasion for the adoption of "socialism" as the official philosophy of a British political party.

By the adoption of an official philosophy and the putting of that philosophy into writing in the Labor Party program of 1918, ideology became a prominent aspect of British politics, and the role of the intellectuals automatically increased in importance. Of course, the adoption of a specifically ideological program by the Labor Party forced the adoption or the exposition of a nonideological ideology by the Conservative Party. It also forced the adoption of a good many measures proposed, or even passed into law, by the Labor Party, and this created a demand for the services of intellectuals both as propagandists and as executors. How far this conversion of the Conservative Party to some of the methods of the Labor Party has gone was made evident after the Conservative debacle of 1945. R. A. Butler, a scion of a great academic dynasty and himself a man of high academic distinction, called on a group of young intellectuals, active politicians, and theorists to remake both the Conservative image and Conservative policy. This imitation of the enemy paid off handsomely in 1951.

Another important reason for extension of the role of intellectuals was the great increase in the number of young men of the H. G. Wells type. Secondary education and university education were now far more general. There were a great many more people who would claim to be intellectuals than in the past, but not so many as to create, as a class, an unemployed and disaffected intelligentsia. The extension of the state services created a demand for university-trained officials of all kinds and the decline of *laissez-faire*, culminating in the abandonment in 1931 of the once sacred doctrine of free trade, made it necessary to find new doctrines to replace the old Benthamite orthodoxy. Then, like all the Western world, Britain was faced first by the Communist and then by the Fascist challenge. Each provided a doctrine and each succeeded in making converts in Britain. But there was a great difference in the importance and value of the converts. Converts to Fascism in Britain were usually very far from being intellectuals, although both William Joyce and Sir Oswald Mosley were persons of remarkable abilities and, so far as Joyce is concerned, of a distinguished academic record.

The appeal of Communism was far more profound. Marxism had been permeating English intellectual life for a generation, although there had been few genuine Marxists among English socialists. (For Scottish, Irish, and Welsh socialists it was easier to be consistent and doctrinaire.) But the Russian Revolution, the depression, and, above all, the rise of Hitler attracted on one side and repelled on the other a great part of the English intellectual class, especially the important class of scientists. They "could not meet a payroll," but they could do a great many things that the most confident payroll-meeter could not do; their role was made immensely more "prestigious" by the events of the Second World War, which still further extended the authority of the state, still further extended the idea of management of the economy, and still further extended the hopes and fears provoked by the advance of the physical sciences. No mere businessmen had the prestige of Keynes, who unkindly pointed out that many or most businessmen who thought they were enunciating truths discovered for themselves were usually repeating the shibboleths of academics of a generation or two in the past! (The fact that Keynes was not only the most brilliant economist of his age but made a great deal of money for himself—and his college—of course added enormously to his prestige.) The debate with Communism as a danger, the debate with the Soviet Union as a source of power, could not be conducted at the mere level of abuse at which it was often conducted in the United States, or by suppressing, or attempting to suppress, dangerous thoughts.

After the Second World War there was again a "crisis of conscience," to use the French phrase which, slowly in some cases and quickly in others, disabused many of the intellectuals with the promises and the performances of the Soviet Union. Yet for a time an innocent belief that Left could speak to Left dominated a great part of the Labor Party. But neither the converts to Communism nor the disabused faithful ever created such a stir as they did in America. Communists and ex-Communists were accepted, often with complete justification, as being more English than Communist. People found it hard to accept a great many of the converts to Communism who were so conspicuously English and often so conspicuously upperclass English, as serious disciples of Lenin. Many remembered that the first prophet of Marxism in England, H. M. Hyndman, was an old Etonian, and it was noted much more recently, with no surprise, that the leader of the Chinese wing of the British Communist Party was the son of a general and an old Etonian. But in any event, the intellectuals' place in political life was taken for granted, and it was a high one. After the retirement of Winston Churchill, three of the four Prime Ministers were men who had graduated with high honors at Oxford. The fourth, Sir Alec Douglas-Hume, did not distinguish himself academically but he had been an outstanding cricketer at Eton, which in England is at least quite as good, even though there are many people who think that Sir Alec's unintellectual character is no longer an asset. It used to be an English term of abuse that X was "too clever by half"; now it has become an English term of abuse that X is "not half clever enough." All the present pretenders to Sir Alec Douglas-Hume's succession have, in fact, had brilliant academic careers.

It would be an exaggeration to say that the rank-and-file of the British political parties are intellectuals or that many leaders, apart from the very top echelons, are of the top rank, either. The House of Representatives, probably, and the United States Senate, certainly, contain a much higher proportion of men who could reasonably be described as intellectuals than does the House of Commons. There is, indeed, a kind of blind reverence for any kind of specialized knowledge in both the United States and Britain, and at times one is inclined to recall Miss Rose Macaulay's gibe at the "not-so-very-intelligentsia." But the intellectuals do play an increasingly important part.

It is now fully accepted that Britain needs brains as well as character. Many old-fashioned Englishmen were shocked to learn that in the negotiations for entry to the Common Market, the French negotiators were at least as competent in modern eco-

SIR DENIS BROGAN

nomic techniques as were the English. The flight of highly educated Englishmen and Scotsmen to America is no longer a matter of "good riddance of bad rubbish" but a subject for national lamentation about the "brain drain." Snobbery, the great English virtue or vice, according to taste, is now on the side of the highbrows. It is only for a short time in youth that being a "square" is a handicap. Being a highly trained and intelligent "square" is the aim of a great part of the brighter youth of both sexes. The leadership in all political parties is more and more in the hands of people of advanced academic training. The Labor Government of 1964 brought into its service a great many persons of varied experience—above all, a great many distinguished academics, many of whom were British by origin. There is hardly any survival in England of the old Jacksonian belief that any good party member is fit for any job. Indeed, "the rise of the meritocracy" is an accepted phenomenon, welcomed by some, hated by others.

"Socialism is about equality" was a famous dictum, but there are more forms than one of inequality. Now it is being argued that the inequality of brains is a more serious grievance than inequality of birth or wealth. After all, the happy accidents of birth and, quite often, of inheritance of wealth, *are* accidental; they do not reflect on people who have not been so lucky, and a great many Englishmen and Englishwomen (I am not so sure about the Scots, the Welsh, and the Irish) are inclined to greet the lucky with a "nice work if you can get it." But inequality of brains is another matter, and if Britain is to be ruled, as is increasingly probable, by a "meritocracy," consisting of persons chosen or self-chosen because of their intellectual ability, there is a danger of a new cleavage as embittering as the old social barriers were and, to a considerable degree, still are.

The differences between the "educated" and the "uneducated" are great and may be growing greater. Everyone, or nearly everyone, is literate. But there are levels in literacy. To get a college education, or at any rate a degree, is not as yet quite as essential as it is in the United States, but then it is a great deal more difficult. And those who do not get it, who do not get the chance to get it, or who fail in the course of getting it, are marked in a way that they very naturally resent.

What are these marks? To an astonishing degree, Britain—especially England—is still inegalitarian in its social tone. The United States is an egalitarian society to an extent quite unknown in England (although it is not as egalitarian as Australia). There are different accents in America: different ways of dressing; schools and colleges have more or less prestige; but none of these things have the importance that they still have in England. Groton is still not Eton; the Ivy League is not Oxbridge. But whereas the old social superiority could sometimes be bridged by common taste— that is, for horse racing, gambling, and other popular activities—the educational and intellectual differences remain insuperable. There is, for example, a very sharp division between what is rather sentimentally called the "quality press" and the popular press. The quality press has quite a small circulation—even the two most famous members of it, the *Times* and the *Guardian*, have less than 300,000 circulation apiece

—but its prestige *inside* the Establishment is very great indeed. The *Economist,* the *New Statesman,* the *Spectator,* have circulation well below 100,000 apiece, but they have far more prestige and, in a sense, far more power than popular sexy weeklies like *Reveille.* Although the late Ellen Wilkinson's innocent ambition to see England a "Third Programme country" has fortunately not been realized, tastes in music, reading matter, and television mark off the classes. As a recent *New Yorker* drawing put it, the absence of television does not prove that someone is an intellectual, but it is a beginning! Moreover, it is beginning to be noticed that with the much greater ease of access to higher education, the working class has its natural leaders siphoned off, instead of going to work for wages, as soon as it was legally possible. The bright working-class boy, if not quite so often the bright working-class girl, goes to secondary school and very often, now, to a university. The union leaders of the past—self-made men of great intrinsic ability like Ernest Bevin, or labor leaders like Aneurin Bevan—are increasingly passing through the higher educational mill and coming out stamped as members of the meritocracy and, in many instances, of the governing class. The leadership of the Labor Party, it is noticed, is more and more one of persons of middle-class origins or, at any rate, middle-class education. (It has, of course, some Etonians as well.)

But, it may be asked, what has this got to do with intellectuals in politics? This is not what the French meant by *intellectuels* in 1900. Few of those mentioned are "idéologues" or Ideologists. Is anyone with a college degree "intellectual"? It is easy to answer the last question in the negative (I am, after all, a college teacher). But the British view of intellectuals is, in fact, an idea of a fairly integrated group of people, most of whom have passed through the higher educational mill—or if, like Winston Churchill, they did not, it is more the fault of the mill than of the men. The English establishment is still essentially integrated, from the French or American point of view. Bishops and generals, lawyers and scientists, painters and musicians, cabinet ministers and publishers overlap far more than they do in New York or Washington or Paris. This, in England, is thought to be a virtue.

Of course, ten or twenty years ago, this group of intellectuals was too narrowly recruited and too small in numbers. Various estimates have been made of its numbers, ranging from two thousand to ten thousand—not many in a population of fifty million! But, of course, today, far more than this small group qualify. It is no longer true that nearly all of the intellectually active in politics and public affairs come from Oxford and Cambridge, live in London or Oxford or Cambridge, are members of one or two of the five or six leading clubs, tend to live in the same parts of London and tend to intermarry. But the English intellectual who is not active in politics is yet likely to have friends who are active in politics of administration or in the new quasi-political jobs such as that of being a director of the Bank of England or the head of a great corporation (it matters little whether it is nationalized or not), or the head of a national institute, or the editor of one of the "quality" newspapers. Raymond Aron, writing in *L'Opium des Intellectuels,* thought that was one of the reasons for the fact that political thought in England is more "with it" than in France. From the English point of view, Pierre-Paul Schweitzer, head of the International Monetary Fund and a highly trained economist who was an active and heroic Resistance leader, is more of a true intellectual in politics than is his cousin Jean-Paul Sartre, however, important Sartre may be as a moral philosopher. There are, of course, plenty of painters, musicians, architects, novelists, and the like in Britain who are in no sense of the term interested in politics. We have our "idiots" as the Greeks had, although we are not quite so contemptuous of them as the Greeks were. But more and more it has come to be accepted that persons of a high degree of intellectual training and, what is often not the same thing, a high degree of intellectual ability and, more rarely still, originality, have a duty to serve the state in some way or other, and it is felt that they best serve the state by using their inherent or acquired abilities in relevant fields. This does not prevent them from having intellectual as well as other hobbies; but politics or, if you like, statecraft, is still in Britain too sacred to be merely a hobby, although it is for many people a hobby as well as a duty. The role of the intellectual in British politics is not as dramatic or as violent as it is in countries in which the intellectual is merely a member of a much larger body of intelligentsia. It is not as dazzling as is the role of a prophet in a country like France, even if the prophet has fewer and fewer faithful when he descends from his mountain to preach practical politics. It may be true—I think it is true—that too much ability goes into government service in Britain and not enough in the United States. But if I had to choose, I should choose the British way. I am, after all, a British intellectual with all the faults and limitations of my class. As Luther said, in a very different context, I cannot do anything else.

WE BEGIN WITH A PROBLEM OF DEFINITION: WHAT DO WE MEAN WHEN we speak of intellectuals in Communist countries? In contemporary Soviet usage, the term "intelligentsia" is officially defined as "a social stratum consisting of people who are occupied professionally with mental labor." It ex-

cludes workers, peasants, and low-level clerical personnel, but among the occupa-
tions included are all managerial personnel in industry, trade, and agriculture; the
Party apparatus; technical personnel in industry and agriculture, including engineers,
architects, technicians, foremen, agronomists, and veterinarians; scientific workers,
physicians and intermediate medical personnel, including midwives, nurses, laboratory workers, and pharmacists; teachers, librarians, journalists, writers, and artists;
economists, accountants, and planners; lawyers, army officers, and students in the
universities and technical institutes.

Obviously, the current Soviet conception of the intelligentsia includes many categories not commonly thought of in non-Communist countries as entitling their members to credentials as intellectuals. At the same time, Soviet definitions go part way
toward accommodating themselves to Western usage by distinguishing between the
technical intelligentsia, which has grown so rapidly in numbers and importance with
industrialization, and the *tvorcheskaya intelligentsia*, or creative intelligentsia of
writers, artists, scholars, and other representatives of the world of culture whose
concerns more closely approximate those of the Western intellectual.

The role of the creative intelligentsia, and, more particularly, the literary intelligentsia, claims attention here. First, it is important to understand the milieu in which
Soviet writers operate. Their assigned task, in the words of the Party program, "lies
in strengthening ties with the life of the people, and in the truthful and highly artistic depiction of the richness and diversity of Socialist reality, in inspired and vivid
portrayal of all that is new and genuinely communist, and exposure of all that hin-
ders the progress of society." Khrushchev, before his downfall, was more explicit.
He pronounced, "The press and radio, literature, painting, music, the cinema and
the theater are a sharp ideological weapon of our Party. The Party is concerned that
its weapon be always in battle readiness and that it hit the enemy accurately. The
Party will allow no one to blunt its edge, to weaken its effect. In questions of creative
art the Party Central Committee will seek to obtain from all—from the most honored
and best known writer or artist and from the young, fledgling creative worker—
unswerving execution of the Party line." His successors have somewhat modified
these strictures. While still insisting that Soviet intellectuals must conform to the
Marxist-Leninist philosophy of dialectical materialism and the principles of Socialist
realism, they have promised that Party controls will be exercised in a less heavy-
handed way. Quoting from a 1925 Central Committee resolution on literature, A. H.
Rumyantsev, editor of *Pravda*, recently declared, "Communist criticism must rid
itself of the tone of literary command. The Party must in every way eradicate attempts
at homebred and incompetent administrative interference in literary affairs."

Rumyantsev's words of encouragement to writers and artists who seek more elbow room to experiment should not be taken to mean that the party is prepared to
abdicate its role as ideological spokesman and guide in literary matters; nor will it
tolerate any form of literary or artistic activity that places its own principles in peril.
In the words of L. F. Ilyichev, the former chairman of the Central Committee's

Ideological Commission, "The question of creative freedom must be fully clari-fied. . . . We have full freedom to fight for Communism. We have not and cannot have freedom to fight against Communism."

The Party possesses a formidable armory of weapons to enforce its views. It can tempt writers to meet its demands by rewarding conformists with large editions, swollen royalty accounts, and the amenities and perquisites these can command. It can punish the deviant and the recalcitrant by subjecting them to public criticism, censoring their output, denying them publication, and, in the most extreme cases, consigning them to prison or exile under the criminal or anti-parasite laws.

But there are also certain things that the Party cannot do. It cannot force a writer to write if he is prepared to shoulder the consequences of not writing. It cannot make talented writers out of hacks, and it has learned more than once that to rely on hacks to transmit its message is to deaden and kill its appeal. It seeks to enlist the creatively gifted in its service but frequently finds itself impaled on the horns of a dilemma where the needs of creativity and conformity clash. The problem the Party faces in engaging the energies of the creative intelligentsia is made dramati-cally manifest in one of Yevtushenko's recent poems. "A Ballad about Poachers" was ostensibly inspired by an item in the Soviet press about the illegal use of small-meshed nets by a fishery collective on the Pechora River in northern Russia. The poem is cast in the form of an appeal by one of the young fish caught in the narrow-mesh nets. He addresses the chairman of the collective:

You've made the mesh too small
your net is illegal. And if it's
    impossible
To live without nets in this world,
Then let them at least
Be legal nets.

Then in an allusion to older, tainted Stalinist writers, Yevtushenko adds:

Old fish have entangled
    themselves
and cannot diseangage themselves.
But young fish are also
    getting entangled.
Why do you destroy the young?
Make the mesh wider.
It's impossibly narrow.
Let the young fool around
Before they become hors d'oeuvre.

And the young fish then comes to the point—

Listen to me, chairman
You're going to make a fool of yourself.
The narrower the mesh,

> The worse it will be for you;
> And even if you succeed
>   in avoiding disgrace
> Say what will you do
> When the Pechora River
>   becomes fishless.

It is precisely this danger that the Pechora River may become fishless that probably inspired Rumyantsev's recent assurance to the intellectuals that they can look forward to a period of wider-meshed nets and greater creative freedom.

Since Stalin's death, the Soviet Union has provided a fascinating laboratory to study the potentialities and limits of intellectual freedom under Communism. The repudiation of the Stalinist legacy of mass terror encouraged the more venturesome among the creative intelligentsia to explore the boundaries of their new freedom and even to function, in the nineteenth-century tradition of their intelligentsia forebears, as critics of the established order. The regime, on the other hand, sought to engage the support of the intelligentsia, while setting limits to its more dangerous critical proclivities. This policy, perhaps best summed up in the ambiguous formula of controlled relaxation, has consisted thus far of alternating phases in which a loosening of bonds has been followed by tighter restrictions which, in turn, have given way to easings of pressure.

To undertand post-Stalinist developments, one needs to view them in the perspective of what went before. The early years after the Revolution were still a period of relative freedom. Party controls were not as rigid as they were later to become. The period of the tightening of controls began with the consolidation of Stalin's power in the late twenties. Literature during those years received its Five Year Plan, along with industry and agriculture. The writers were now christened "engineers of the human soul," and they had their set themes and their set goals. With the organization of the Union of Soviet Writers in 1934, controls became even more sweeping. Writers were expected to serve the Party cause and glorify Stalin. This was the predominant line down to the war and the Nazi attack on the Soviet Union in June 1941.

The war period opened up new possibilities for the writers. There was less stress on the party and more on patriotic-national themes that would have an inclusive appeal. The necessities of the Alliance bred more tolerance of cosmopolitan interests, and the sufferings of the war were also permitted an outlet in the form of deeply personal poetry that had little or nothing to do with glorification of the Party or of Stalin. One of the most popular of the war poems was Konstantin Simonov's "Wait for Me" (1941); a few stanzas will convey its flavor:

> Just wait for me and I'll return
> But wait, Oh wait, with all your might . . .
> Wait when your heart is saddened by
> The pouring rains, the sallow light.

Wait when the wind heaps up the snow,
Wait when the air is dry and hot.
Wait when the rest no longer wait
For those whom they too soon forgot.
Wait when the letters fail to come,
Wait on, through dread and through despair, . . .
Just wait for me and I'll return.
And show no kindliness to such
As know by heart that it is time
To cease from grieving over much.
Let both my mother and my son
Believe me lost, let friends who tire
Of waiting sit them down
Barren of hope beside the fire,
And let them toast my memory
In bitter wine as friends will do.
Wait. While they drink, be waiting still,
Nor lift the glass they pour for you . . .
Just wait for me and I'll return.

This was the kind of poetry that touched the hearts of millions, and it contained not a word about Party, State, or Stalin.

As the war drew to a close and victory was within grasp, a mood of demobilization set in. After the grim hardships, people longed to relax, to taste the joys of victory and peace, and to lead an easier life. This, too, found its expression in literature, in poems such as Surkov's "Evening." He sang:

And after victory we will make a halt
Drink a cup, and rest to our heart's content.

But it was not to be. Stalin was not interested in demobilization. The end of the war was marked by a tightening of Party controls; there was no room for poems expressing longing for the beloved, for relaxation, pleasure, and joy.

The Party entered the fray with the Central Committee resolution of May 14, 1946, on the journals *Zvenda* and *Leningrad*. The speeches of Zhdanov, the new cultural Tsar, which accompanied the decree, marked a vigorous reassertion of the Party's role in literature. Said Zhdanov:

". . . Any preaching of ideological neutrality, of political neutrality, of Art for Art's sake is alien to Soviet literature and harmful to the interests of the Soviet people and to the Soviet state. Such preaching has no place in our journals. . . . The task of Soviet literature is to aid the state to educate the youth correctly and to meet their demands, to rear a new generation strong and vigorous, believing in their cause, fearing no obstacles and ready to overcome all obstacles."

Soviet literature, said Zhdanov, must concern itself with current themes, inculcate loyalty to Party and state, attack bourgeois culture, show Soviet man as positive and

MERLE FAINSOD

optimistic, and educate the youth to be cheerful, confident in its own strength, and unafraid of any difficulties. The Zhdanov pronouncements threw the literary world into a turmoil. They were marked by ugly attacks on many writers, including such talented figures as Anna Akhmatova and Michail Zoshchenko. Some stopped writing, while others adjusted and conformed by writing made-to-order novels, plays, and poems without any literary merit. The *Zhdanovshchina*, as it was called, cast a dark blight on Soviet literature, which lasted, with some slight moderation after 1949, until Stalin's death.

After this occurrence, came The Thaw, with its promises of a better life to come, of an end to mass terror and of more attention to man and his well-being. The writers began to revive their courage and explore new themes. Some were courageous indeed. The poet Alexander Tvardovsky, himself a high-ranking Party member, helped to set the new mood with his satire of the Zhdanov made-to-order novel:

> Here's your novel, all in order,
> Showing the new bricklaying method,
> The backward assistant director, the pro-
>   gressive chairman,
> The old granddad marching to Communism.
> He and she—outstanding workers—
> The motor installed and started,
> The Party organizer, the storm, the breakdown,
>   the emergency,
> The Minister visits the shops—then the big
>   party.
> All suggesting, all resembling
> What is or might be,
> But, when added up, so indigestible
> That one feels like screaming.

Two other works, L. Zorin's play *The Guests* and Ilya Ehrenburg's novelette *The Thaw,* may serve to illustrate the new notes that were being struck in the immediate post-Stalinist years. Zorin's play is essentially a study in generations: the grandfather a hero of the revolution who lives austerely and retains his ideals; the son, a high-ranking bureaucrat remote from the people, poisoned by power, and leading a "gluttonous" life as a member of the new Soviet state bourgeoisie; the grandson, sharing the values of his father and accepting all the amenities which he has inherited as his due. One sees the outlines of a new privileged class emerging. This is apparent, too, in Ehrenburg's *The Thaw,* in which the principal negative character, Zhuravlyov, a factory director, is portrayed as narrow and self-seeking, neglecting the welfare of his workers and using whatever means are at his disposal to advance his own career. Running through Ehrenburg's story is a recurring note of discontent with Soviet society and the cultural values which pervade it. In the words of one of his characters: "We have taken a lot of trouble over one half of the human being, but the other half is neglected. The result is that one half of the house is a slum. I remember that article of Gorky's I read long ago, while I was still at school; he said we needed our own Soviet humanism. The word has been forgotten, the task is still to be done. In those days it was only a presentiment, now it's time we tackled it." Speaking through the mouth of another of his characters, Volodya, a disillusioned and cynical hack painter, Ehrenburg has this to say: "Raphael wouldn't be admitted to the Artists' Union. . . . Everybody's shouting about art and nobody cares a fig for it really; that's the sign of our time." Volodya is equally critical of the content of Soviet literature. A writer, he points out, is not expected to have ideas. "What you're meant to look for in a book is ideology. If it's there what more do you want. It's lunatics that have ideas."

All this was too much. Zorin's attack on the New Privileged Class and Ehrenburg's pessimistic picture of the cultural values of Soviet society touched tender spots; by mid-1954 chill winds began to blow again. The writers seemed to be getting out of hand, and it was necessary to discipline them. The Second All-Union Writers' Congress, which opened on December 15, 1954, was designed to bring the writers back into line. It was not altogether successful. The congress' proceedings were marked by sharp attacks on the bureaucrats who ran the writers' organization; on the whole, the organizers of the congress were on the defensive. There was a noticeable absence of forceful guidance; indeed, the Party spokesmen at the congress, while denouncing Zorin and his ilk, tried to occupy middle ground. In effect, their message was this: we don't want to go back to the worst excesses and rigid doctrinarism of the Zhdanov era, but at the same time the writers must behave. They must realize that their literary output must serve the interests of the Party. During the next year (1955), the Party controllers of literature tried to enforce this uneasy compromise. They enjoyed only moderate success. It was clear that beneath the surface there was a great deal of resentment among some of the better writers against this new effort to tighten the bonds.

Then came the Twentieth Party Congress in 1956 and Khrushchev's dramatic attack on Stalin. A number of writers interpreted this as the signal for a new era of liberalism and bold new themes began to be aired. Real criticism of some of the more unsavory aspects of Soviet reality began to find its way into literature; some of the most sacrosanct features of the regime were openly challenged and condemned.

What were these themes? First, there was a continuation of the attack on the privileges of the New Class of Party and state bureaucrats. Second, there was an attempt to escape the compulsions of the political by retreating into a world of private and personal concerns. Third, there was a revolt against what the Russians call *lakirovka*, against varnishing and prettifying Soviet reality, which expressed itself in a passion for truth and for the tearing away of masks. And, finally, there was a new stress on humanitarian values, on the need to respect people and to treat them decently, on a call for courageous people who will speak up and fight for their rights, on the need for compassion and the airing of a deep sorrow for the harshnesses and injustices of Soviet life.

Let me illustrate these themes as they found expression in Soviet literature after the Twentieth Party Congress. Vladimir Dudintsev's novel *Not by Bread Alone* may serve as an example of the attack on the New Class. What gave the novel its sense of urgency was not its rather shopworn plot of the inventor who struggles for recognition against bureaucratic opposition but rather the sharpness of its criticism of the bureaucracy as a home of narrow-minded, unprincipled self-seekers concerned primarily with their comforts and their careers. These qualities were summed up in the character called Drozdov, who was portrayed as a typical member of the class.

The novel quickly became a subject of controversy, and the discussion it inspired touched on some of the most sensitive areas of Soviet life. At a public meeting in the Moscow writers' club in October 1956, Konstantin Paustovsky, one of the most respected of the older generation of Soviet writers, rose to Dudintsev's defense and was rebuked for his pains. The cautious summary of his remarks in *Literaturnaya Gazeta* (Literary Gazette) read: "K. Paustovsky went on to tell of his trip to Europe on the liner Pobeda, on which he chanced to meet with certain 'responsible' workers who, in his opinion, are akin to Drozdov. From these observations K. Paustovsky drew a series of incorrect conclusions and generalizations to the effect that Drozdovs are a mass phenomenon." The full text of Paustovsky's speech, not published in the Soviet Union, was transcribed at the meeting and subsequently appeared in *L'Express*, in France. It was an amazingly frank denunciation of bureaucratic philistinism. Charging that there were "thousands of Drozdovs" still around, he illustrated their vulgarity and arrogance with descriptions of their behavior on the European tour. Paustovsky continued: "This is not merely a matter of describing a few careerists. It's not simply a matter of careerists. It's all much more complex and more important than that. The problem is that in our country a completely new social stratum exists with impunity and even flourishes up to a certain point—a new petty bourgeois caste. It is a new population of rapacious and propertied persons who have nothing in common with the Revolution, with our regime, or with Socialism." He then went on to charge them with having served as Stalin's hatchetmen. "If it weren't for the Drozdovs, such people as Meyerhold, Babel, Artyon Vesyoly, and many others would still be living among us. They were destroyed by the Drozdovs. And they were destroyed in the name of the stinking comfort of these Drozdovs."

Dudintsev and Paustovsky were not alone in directing their fires at the New Class. One of the most moving documents of this period was Nikolai Zhdanov's story "A Visit Home," which appeared in *Literaturnaya Moskva* early in 1957.* It attacks the great gulf which exists between kolkhoz peasants and Party officials. The story describes how a busy official, now a big shot, returns to his native village to attend his mother's funeral. It is many years since he has been there, and he finds the villagers living in great poverty. The visitor is deeply depressed, most of all when one of the

---

* An English translation of this story appears in *Bitter Harvest* (New York: Praeger, 1959).

women of the kolkhoz, a soldier's wife, half-apologetically describes how things are to him, a former villager but now a Man from the Center, who presumably can do something about the situation.

"I wanted to ask you," she says, "have they done right by us here? This year we sowed seventy-four acres with hemp. It was just ready when the summer wheat also got ripe for cutting. We should have gathered the hemp, but they ordered us to thresh the grain deliveries and take the grain to the collection center. You know, if you don't do the hemp in time, you lose it, but they wouldn't listen to us; they wanted their grain deliveries and that was that. . . . And so we lost the hemp. And now we've no bread again. Now tell me, is that good or not?"

"She thinks it all depends on me," says the official to himself. And out loud, he answers importantly, "That is a political question. The State must always come first. Everything depends on the level of consciousness of the masses." He's not at all satisfied with his explanation, but the peasant woman looks pleased and he thinks, "She is happy because the conversation has reached a high level." But the official's conscience gnaws at him; he can't face the misery of the people. He longs to escape back to his comfortable office in Moscow, and at the end of the story we see him on the train going back to Moscow, half-dozing in his compartment, unable to fall asleep, still thinking about the village. He begins to dream uneasily. He sees his village again. He sees his mother as he saw her being buried, her face small and dark as she bends toward him, expectant and hopeful, and she asks, as the soldier's wife had asked, "Have they done right by us here?"

Here is still another story—really more a sketch than a story—Yuri Nagibin's "The Light in the Window." In a convalescent home, a suite of rooms has for years been kept in readiness for a Very Important Person, who never comes. Day after day, the rooms are thoroughly cleaned by a woman especially hired for the job; even when the home is jammed full these rooms are not used. One fine day the cleaning woman breaks the regulations. She and the porter and his children all sit down in the luxurious room and they turn on its new television set, to the speechless horror of the director, who sees them through the window. In a single act of indiscipline, the cleaning woman sweeps aside the barrier erected between "them"—the New Class—and the people.

This is literature teaching a new kind of moral; the political symbolism of the story is daring, almost a call to revolt. Not surprisingly, the writer soon found himself under sharp attack.

Side by side with these strictures directed against the state bourgeoisie there also emerged an apolitical literary trend, a turn away from politics to personal concerns, love, family, marriage, and its problems. A popular play by Alyoshin called *Odna* (Alone) may serve as an example. The plot of the play is simple. A middle-aged engineer, married for sixteen years to an attractive schoolteacher and with a teen-age daughter, becomes hopelessly infatuated with the beautiful wife of a younger colleague. She also falls madly in love with him. They try to fight their love for each other, but in the end they surrender to it. The beautiful young wife leaves her husband; the engineer abandons his wife and child. There is no happy ending. At the conclusion of the play, the abandoned wife simply proclaims her faith that, despite all that has happened, one must try to go on living, one must live decently, and try to fulfill one's capacities.

To understand the excitement and controversy which this play aroused, one must appreciate how far removed it was from the usual political morality play served up to the Russian theatergoer in Moscow. There was no typology, nor were there clearly demarcated positive and negative heroes. All the parties concerned were portrayed as decent people betrayed by their emotions; all acted as human beings, with all their frailties. Western audiences would hardly regard the play as shocking. For Soviet audiences it was new, and they found themselves caught up in what seemed a daring and frank confrontation of an eternal human problem rather than a Party message.

Still other recurrent themes were the protest against prettifying Soviety reality and the call for a new humanism. These received particularly forceful expression in the works of the younger poets. Here, for example, are some lines from a poem by Robert Rozhdestvensky, in which he addresses himself to the threat of a revival of Stalinism:

> Be silent, night. You cannot cry down
> The dawn which now lights half the heaven.
> He who conceals his sickness must die.
> You say that in your light the dirt cannot be
> seen?
> We want to see it.
> Do you hear? It is time.

Or again, in the words of farewell which Yevtushenko's native Siberian village, Stantsiya Zima (Winter Station), speaks to him:

> Seek, seek. Roam the whole wide world.
> Yes, truth is good, and happiness is better.
> But still without truth, there can be no happiness.
> Go into the world, holding your head high,
> Looking always forward—with heart and eyes,
> But on your face—
> The look of wet pine needles,
> And on your eyelashes—
> Tears and storm.
> Love people—and you will understand them.
> Remember—
> I shall be watching you.
> It will be hard—and you will return to me—
> Now go!
> And I went.
> And so I go.

The Role of Intellectuals in the Soviet Union   83

These were the themes of 1956—love people; seek the truth; let us have a personal life again; we're fed up with the privileges of the bureaucracy. As can be imagined, they were not very palatable to the Party leadership. Genuinely shocked and outraged by the unintended consequences of de-Stalinization—the Hungarian revolt, the Polish October, and the intellectual ferment in the Soviet Union—the regime replied in a not unfamiliar pattern: with force in Hungary, with suspicion and reluctant acquiescence in Poland, and with a renewed war on "unhealthy" ideological manifestations in the Soviet Union. After Hungary, the swing of the cultural pendulum moved for a time in a neo-Stalinist direction. The more restive spirits among the Soviet literary intelligentsia were subjected to sharp criticism, called upon to recant, and summoned to meetings to confess their sins.

But some of them were stubborn. They refused to confess their errors and when called upon to speak they said nothing. This led the Party bureaucrats to charge that the writers had joined in what they called a conspiracy of silence. L. Sobolev, one of the most orthodox of the non-Party writers, expressed the regime's concern. Addressing those who had remained silent, he said:

"Your silence is dangerous. It causes disorientation among the readers. What does it mean? What does it conceal? An arrogant contempt for the opinion of others? A contemptuous belief in one's own infallibility. An insulting 'How could you possibly understand us?' The pathos of readiness for sacrifice? What does this silence signify? We do not understand it. Neither does the people. Do you know what became known to me yesterday and what shocked me, so that I felt compelled to mount the platform and excite myself beyond the measures permitted by my physician? That in the Western press hypocritically friendly sentiments are being voiced concerning you, you who should speak today but do not. That a 'friendly' [Western] hand is being extended towards you. That they are ready to embrace you, that a rope is ready for you that would draw you even further from your own people? Do you know that you are being enjoined to commit 'the heroic act of being silent'? The heroics of silence? What strange and poisonous world. . . ." And Sobolev concluded his speech with the fervent hope that the writers would not follow this diabolic advice from the West.

Then came pressure and discipline (though not arrests), and finally the heavy artillery of Khrushchev himself was mobilized to lay down the line. Essentially, Khrushchev's message was this: you must not slander Soviet reality; you must write about the favorable aspects of Soviet life. One may expose the shortcomings and mistakes of individuals, but one cannot attack or challenge the Soviet order itself. All literature must adhere to Party positions, celebrate the nobility of labor, and arouse the people to struggle for new victories in the building of Communism.

Some writers obliged. There was a new rash of official, made-to-order novels, such as Kochetov's *The Brothers Yershov*. But the drive toward orthodoxy also met with resistance. Despite the favor shown by the regime to such untalented official hacks as Kochetov, despite Khrushchev's warnings at a series of receptions for writers that they must follow Party directives, and despite the campaign launched against Pasternak for defying the ban on the publication of *Dr. Zhivago*, a number of writers continued to maintain courageous independent positions, and it was one of the most talented of them, Andrei Voznesensky, who wrote, on the occasion of Pasternak's death:

> They bore him to no entombment
> They bore him to enthronement.

At the Third Writers' Congress, in 1959, Khrushchev called on the writers to settle their own quarrels. Despite this summons, the breach widened between the old-line conformists and the writers pressing for greater creative freedom. It received open expression at the Twenty-Second Party Congress in 1961, when Kochetov spoke for the Old Guard and Tvardovsky for the liberals. In the aftermath of the Twenty-Second Party Congress, with the renewal of the assault on Stalinism, it appeared for a time that the liberals were carrying the day. There was a new upsurge of hope, a new outburst of critical realism. Thus Yevtushenko, in his poem "Stalin's Heirs," called for a sharp break with the Stalinist past:

> And I appeal to our government
> With the request
> To double,
> To triple
>   The guard at this slab
> So that Stalin may not rise
> And, with Stalin
>   the past
>
> . . . .
>
> I mean by the past
> The ignoring of the people's welfare
>   The calumnies
>   The arrests of the innocent

And, noting that there were little Stalins still around, he continued:

> [They] even condemn Stalin from the platform,
> But themselves
>   at night
> pine for the old days
>
> . . . .
>
> They, once his lieutenants,
>   Do not like these times
> When the camps are empty
>   And the halls where people listen to poetry
>   Are crowded. . .

Another poet, Rozhdestvensky, in his poem "Motherland" spoke out for the right of youth to think for itself:

And don't dare try
     to persuade us stealthily
Adopting enigmatic poses;
It's too early for you,
     lads,
       to understand
         all that . . .
Early?
Better early
     than late!
We will no longer say:
     Someone
       is thinking
        for us!
We've found out
     what that
       ends with!

Writers hastened to exploit the theme of the conflict of the generations. Perhaps the most talented work in this genre was Vasili Aksenov's novel *Ticket to the Stars,* which was published in 1961 and provided a remarkably outspoken airing of the desire on the part of at least some young people to be free to find their own way in life without constant tutelage and official direction.

Perhaps the most powerful work of this period was Alexander Solzhenitsyn's description of life in a concentration camp, *One Day in the Life of Ivan Denisovich,* which was published with Khrushchev's personal blessing, but which in turn unleashed a flood of concentration-camp literature that Khrushchev undertook to check by warning that the theme was a delicate one. In the same critical vein as Solzhenitsyn's novel, though less talented, was Fyodor Abramov's *Round and About,* a frank exposure of the lack of interest of collective farmers in kolkhoz work and a plea for dealing with the problem of improving incentives. An equally unorthodox note was struck by the novelist Nekrasov, whose objective account in *Novy Mir* of his travels in Italy and America laid him open to the charge of having failed to display the necessary ideological militancy in dealing with bourgeois phenomena. The literary ferment which both preceded and followed the Twenty-Second Congress enlisted some of the most creative voices in the younger and middle generations—such poets as Yevtushenko, Voznesensky, and Akmadullina, and such talented writers of fiction as Aksenov, Kazakov, Nagibin, Nekrasov, and Solzhenitsyn. They numbered among their supporters such respected elder literary figures as Tvardovsky, Ehrenburg, and Paustovsky.

But this time, too, high hopes met frustration. The crackdown began when Khrushchev visited the Manege exhibition in Moscow on December 1, 1962, and singled out the abstract art on exhibition for his now famous dictum "Such pictures were not painted by the hand of man but by the tail of a donkey!" From painting and sculpture the attack spread to music and literature. Artists, composers, and writers were accused of producing "formalist monstrosities" alien to the people. Nor were the criticisms limited to style and form. Members of the "liberal" group were also accused of besmirching Soviet reality, of failing to defend correct Party positions, of setting themselves up as representatives of the youth against the Party, and even of giving comfort to the enemy. During the next months, the forces of orthodox conformity gave every appearance of being in the saddle, and they joined in a chorus of full-throated denunciation of their liberal rivals.

But appearances turned out to be deceptive. By May 1963, there were already signs that the conservative campaign had spent its force. Tvardovsky, one of the leaders of the liberal forces, not only retained his editorship of *Novy Mir*, but in a noteworthy interview with Henry Schapiro, the United Press-International correspondent in Moscow, which was published in *Pravda* on May 12, 1963, he was able to indicate in an authoritative manner that his cause was far from lost. The Central Committee plenum on ideology which followed in June, while providing a forum for severe criticism of such recalcitrant writers as Nekrasov, stopped short of a heresy hunt. The turning of the tide became more evident in August, when Khrushchev invited Tvardovsky to read his new poem, "Vasili Tyorkin in the Other World," at a reception for foreign writers. The poem itself, as outspoken an attack on the cant and humbug of the Stalinist era as has yet appeared in the Soviet press, was a clear indication that the conservatives would no longer have a clear field to themselves. The rehabilitation of such writers as Voznesensky and Yevtushenko was quick to follow, and though their first works to see the light of day after their disgrace revealed that they had been chastened by their experience, they at least had a public platform again. In the wake of Khrushchev's removal, there were further signs of liberalization. The publication of Ilya Ehrenburg's memoirs, which had been suspended in 1963, was resumed. New poems and short prose pieces by Boris Pasternak were printed in *Novy Mir*. The same magazine, still under Tvardovsky's editorship, provided a home for such controversial writers as Nekrasov, Yefim Dorosh, and Yevtushenko. The swing of the pendulum pointed, at least temporarily, toward some easing of literary controls.

As one looks back on the cultural history of the Soviet Union since the death of Stalin, with its alternating phases of restriction and relaxation, what is most striking is the continued pressure of the more talented writers for greater creative opportunities. One can almost feel them rediscovering their heritage, edging their way toward greater freedom, and becoming, in the grand tradition of the Russian intelligentsia, the voice of conscience against the rulers of society.

Yet it would be profoundly misleading to conclude that the bulk of the so-called liberal wing of the creative intelligentsia is in open rebellion against the Soviet system. There are, of course, isolated heretics who are completely alienated and disillusioned, who write for the drawer, and whose works are not, and cannot be, published. But the goals of the great majority of the so-called "liberals" are more modest. Running through most of the literature which articulates their spirit of protest is a desire for more independence, a search for fresh forms, a distaste for embellishment, a passion for truth, and a concern with the personal life of man. But those who express these values also consider themselves good Soviet patriots, loyal to the Communist cause as they understand it. If there is a political program concealed in the interstices of their collective works, it is essentially a plea for a more libertarian form of Communism. They do not undertake to present a direct challenge to the system itself.

In this respect the case of Yevtushenko is instructive. A handsome poet of modest talent, he has played a tremendous role as a symbol of youth's discontent. His outlook on the world and his almost Messianic attraction for many Soviet young people provide a fascinating mirror of the complexity of their beliefs and aspirations. On the one hand, he shares with them many attitudes which are politically unexceptionable. His patriotic poems, his poems of praise for Castro's Cuba (which he sees as a symbol of the pure uncorrupted revolution), his denunciation of Fascism, his anti-Stalinism and neo-Leninism not only win official approval but give every appearance of reflecting his own sincere beliefs as well as those of his youthful auditors. On the other hand, much of his appeal to the more restive spirits among the youth derives from the fact that he bursts the bonds of the prescribed orthodoxies. His highly subjective and even erotic poems, his defense of so-called nihilists and beatniks, his openly expressed admiration for abstract art, his calls for the right to travel ("I'm irked by national borders"), his courageous denunciation of Soviet anti-Semitism in the poem "Babi Yar," and his insistence on the right of youth to make mistakes all find support in a generation seeking more elbow room to express its own individuality. But beyond these relatively mild heterodoxies, there are other dimensions of Yevtushenko's outlook which border on open defiance of the regime's values. They include declarations in the course of his travels abroad that he did not believe that capitalism was "going downhill" and that both East and West had "their failings and unhealthy phenomena," and, finally, the very un-class-conscious pronouncement in his autobiography that "I loathe nationalism. For me the entire world is composed of two nations only: that of good men and that of bad men." Such heresies explain the massive effort to discredit him which was launched in early 1963, and it is a measure of his fortitude that, though attacked and disciplined, he could still proclaim:

> I am not accustomed to stooping—
> I have preserved my pride
> And misfortune will not
> Knock me off my feet.

Yevtushenko provides an index of the kind of problem which the more rebellious young intellectuals present for the regime. Despite pampering and special privileges, trips abroad, and large editions, he still overstepped the bounds of approved conduct and invited forms of repressive control which the Party leaders would probably have preferred to avoid if they could have achieved their objectives by other means. In the conservative Kochetov's most recent novel, *Secretary of the Obkom,* the obkom secretary Denisov, described in the novel as a "leader of the new type," observes that the younger generation has "higher demands in everything" than its elders and that "one must work with it more cleverly . . . , without didacticism and shouting; it must be attracted, led, but not shoved around."

It is a prescription which is not easy to enforce. With every relaxation of discipline, new heterodoxies are opened. The very fact that so many of the most talented of the younger (as well as some of the older) literary figures have rallied to the so-called "liberal" banner immensely complicates the task of control. Desirous of using their talent, the regime still cannot give them their head. It alternates between phases of liberalization and of tightened controls because no more effective way of harnessing their energies lies ready at hand. Meanwhile, there is always the danger that this form of manipulation will alienate the so-called liberals and turn loyal oppositionists into enemies of the regime.

The creative intellectual in any society is a special breed that cannot be easily haltered. He seeks outlets for his creativity, and if outlets are closed, he ceases to function. A very talented writer, E. I. Zamyatin, who fled Russia in the twenties, once said, "The best way to kill art is to canonize one form and one philosophy." And on another occasion he wrote, "The main thing is that there can be a real literature only where it is produced by madmen, hermits, heretics, dreamers, rebels, and skeptics, and not by painstaking and well-meaning officials." In the Soviet Union today, the officials are still in the saddle, but it remains to be seen whether the voices of the heretics, dreamers, rebels, and skeptics can be permanently stilled. It was Jean Cocteau who said, "It is the dictators of art who make possible the disobedience without which art dies." What has been happening on the Soviet literary scene since Stalin's death may serve as a reminder that both disobedience and literature are still alive.

W HILE IN HONG KONG, I RECEIVED AN INVITATION TO TAKE PART IN THE conference for which this paper was prepared. As I had planned to visit the United States on my way home to Europe, I accepted the request to substitute for Carlo Schmid, who was prevented by illness from attending.

Constantly on the road, I was unable to reread what some of my countrymen have written on the subject—the late Theodor Heuss, for example, truly an intellectual in politics, a highly cultured man of letters, a successful writer of many books, and the first president of the German Federal Republic after 1949; or Eugen Gerstenmaier, holder of two doctorates—of divinity and philosophy—, a profound thinker, one of the most successful speakers on historical and sociological issues in Germany today, and the president of the Bundestag in Bonn; or Carlo Schmid himself, professor of law, a known connoisseur of literature, translator of Baudelaire, and vice-president of the Bundestag. These three, incidentally, represent the three parties in the Bundestag: Heuss, the Free Democrats; Gerstenmaier, the Christian Democrats, and Schmid, the Social Democrats. Since there was, at the conference, some bragging about the role of the Scots among the British intellectuals, I may be forgiven for bragging, too! These three all came from my part of Germany—from Schwaben (or Württemberg), which for centuries has contributed greatly to the intellectual life of our country.

KEEP AWAY FROM POLITICS

However, even had I reread the pertinent writings of these men, it would not have helped me very much; for I shall present a point of view quite different from that of Carlo Schmid or the other two. Schmid's thesis would have been that intellectuals should go into politics, and he has stated it many times. No wonder—he is an intellectual in politics himself, hence his thesis is an *apologia pro vita sua.* On the other hand, I am an intellectual who has not gone into politics; my advice, therefore, is that intellectuals should stay out of politics, which is, of course, an *apologia pro vita mea.* I shall, therefore, state my thesis with emphasis, hoping that I shall not hurt the feelings of those who are intellectuals *and* in politics.

No agreed-upon definition of the word "intellectual" exists; thus, each of us has to make clear what he means by it. To me, an intellectual is not the same as an "educated person," as some have suggested. Rather—and this is a narrowing of the meaning— an intellectual is one who is primarily preoccupied with three principles: the search for truth, the dedication to humanism, and the struggle for liberty. ("Humanism," in my understanding, refers both to the individual human and to collective humanity; all too often, people who talk of humanism think only of an abstract humanity and neglect the concrete human being.)

And "politics"? This word, too, requires definition. A man in politics is, I suggest, one who makes political decisions, who acts upon his own responsibility in the political field, a person with a drive and a sense for power. This is the kind of politics that intellectuals should shun, for all their virtues as intellectuals turn into vices—or at least, handicaps—if they enter the arena of power politics. In particular, the sense of timing peculiar to the intellectual does not recommend him for political action, since one of his characteristics is that he looks at everything from all sides. A problem may have a hundred aspects, but while the intellectual may be only half through contemplating them, the time for decision has passed, and if he has not been able to make up his mind in time he is too late.

Or—perhaps still oftener—he is too early: he has learned to think ahead, to draw conclusions which though they might be logically correct are practically premature, since logic operates on a level where a step can be taken in a second, while the same step, in the world of politics, may require years. Leon Trotsky for this very reason repeatedly suffered reverses; he produced ideas far in advance of the time that was ripe for their practical application. These ideas were applied later—after Trotsky himself had moved on to new theoretical positions—by others, *i.e.* the New Economic Policy by Lenin, the militarization of labor by Stalin.

Let me mention some great names in recent world politics: Adenauer, for example. I name him not because he is, like me, a German, but because he illustrates very clearly what I mean. Konrad Adenauer, chancellor of the Federal Republic of Germany from 1949 to 1963, is anything but an intellectual; as do many politicians, he even entertains a good deal of suspicion of intellectuals.

Adenauer's political strength—apart from his unusual tactical skill—lay mainly in the relative simplicity of his mind. At a time when most Germans were furiously debating the pros and cons of alternate political roads for West Germany, he had decided that by far the best road would be Germany's integration into the community of the Western nations, with all the consequences this entailed (including the strengthening of the division between West and East Germany). After that, he moved, without wavering and without ever becoming confused by the often rather involved reasoning of his opponents, along this road, and eventually he won the nation to this course—even the Social Democratic opposition party. His *political* alertness was extraordinary and never slackened, even in old age; his interest in purely *intellectual* pursuits was almost nil.

Churchill was a great statesman, as is De Gaulle, but to neither, in any sense of the word, may one attribute the qualities of an intellectual, although each possessed a superb knowledge of how to use the word and the pen. Khrushchev was a politician of the purest water, a master on the political stage despite his many failures and final defeat; but surely he is no intellectual, not even an "educated person," but a self-made man, with a rather late and haphazard education.

Some might, at this point, interject, "But Kennedy!" No doubt, John F. Kennedy was one of the most intelligent politicians in modern times, but I would not call him an intellectual, although he surrounded himself with intellectuals.

Among the great statesman of recent times, Nehru came nearest to being an intellectual; as a statesman, he might have failed for that very reason had he not been carried along by the strong personal *charisma* inherited from Gandhi and by the eager enthusiasm of a nation just freed from colonial domination, willing to follow the lead of the man whom it identified with the struggle for independence. There is also the peculiar way in which the Indians carry over their strong spiritual aspirations even into politics.

KLAUS MEHNERT

As a rule, it seems to me, the politician wins over the intellectual when it comes to politics: the ruthless tactician Lenin over theoreticians such as Plekhanov and Martov; the tough and wholly unintellectual Stalin over the brilliant Trotsky, or Napoleon over the intellectuals of the French Revolution.

My suggestion that the intellectual should stay away from active participation in power politics does not mean that he should stay away from politics altogether. On the contrary, it is my contention that the intellectual should participate in politics—indirectly, not directly, and with the means appropriate to him. He should influence, not make, politics.

THE INDIRECT METHODS

Two possibilities exist for the intellectual to affect the course of events. One is through expertise of one kind or another. A diplomat, for example, may very well be an intellectual putting his intelligence at the service of his government. An intellectual may serve as an adviser. The classic examples of such indirect influence on politics are the brain trusts of Franklin D. Roosevelt and of John F. Kennedy. There was never a question of who was boss—it was the man who called, employed, and used the brain trust and who dominated its members from beginning to end. Even when they ghostwrote his speeches, he was the master of the show. Of this very obvious and well-known type of intellectual influence upon the course of politics I do not write here.

It is, rather, the other method of indirect influence that concerns us now. I call it the way of the weather maker. This term I have taken from a story by Hermann Hesse, one of the major German writers of this century. In his old age, Hesse wrote a lengthy novel, *The Game of Glass Beads*, which deals very much with the subject being discussed here. He described a utopian state, Castalia, ruled by philosophers whose pastime is a difficult and sophisticated game played with glass beads. Hesse has woven into the novel a story about a weather maker of olden days. After learning the trade from the preceding weather maker of the tribe, this man had acquired, following a lifetime of observation and experience, the ability to sense the course of the weather, to predict it, in some cases even to change it. He was the medicine man, the *shaman* of his tribe, not its chief. But, in his way, he was just as important to the tribe, for the chief ruled within the climate the weather maker predicted and shaped.

Karl Marx once said that until his time philosophers had merely interpreted history: he was going to change it. In this statement Marx was of course mistaken. Countless philosophers have influenced, and thus changed, human history: Plato and Aristotle, to name two of the outstanding ancients; or Rousseau—or, in America, John Dewey. These men either did not participate actively in politics at all, or failed when they tried to do so, as was the case with Plato and Marx, but their indirect influence on politics was tremendous; they felt and anticipated the political current, they analyzed and interpreted it, and thus they shaped its future course.

The present-day United States offers a good example of what I mean. In this country are thousands of persons (columnists, writers, commentators, professors, clergymen, and others) who by their ideas constantly exercise a strong influence on the men in Washington. What these people think and say through their page-sized political advertisements in the large newspapers, in their columns or on television, reaches the politically interested part of the population and, through them, the Congress and the Administration. Many a presidential speech or decision has come about in this way. An example of this was the Baltimore speech of President Johnson in April of 1965 on the war in Viet Nam. I do not mean to say that the statesmen are creatures of public opinion—they would be poor statesmen if they were—but I do contend that they are being influenced by public opinion and this is shaped to a large extent by the nation's intellectuals.

GERMANY'S FATEFUL DEVIATION—NATIONALISM

An intellectual must be devoted to the ideals of truth, humanism, and liberty. If he ceases serving these, or if he deviates from them, he ceases to deserve this title and loses his beneficial function. Germany might serve as an example to prove this point. In her Golden Age, during the latter part of the eighteenth and earlier part of the nineteenth, her intellectuals were dedicated to those three ideals: Lessing (whose play "Emilia Galotti" was presented on the University of Texas campus recently), Goethe and Schiller, Kant—and I would include him—Hegel. But then two deviations occurred—one toward nationalism, one toward materialism.

From Treitschke, the historian, to Moeller van den Bruck, the visionary who in the title of one of his books coined the term *Das dritte Reich,* innumerable German intellectuals promoted their country's nationalism, extolling the German nation, its special mission and virtue. This current, grown from the wars of liberation against Napoleon and from the struggle for unification under Bismarck, was emphasized by the nationalist teachings of many German historians and writers of the age, becoming so strong that even a man whom many consider a consistent and unswerving foe of nationalism—the novelist Thomas Mann—fell under its sway, as can be seen in his *Betrachtungen eines Unpolitischen.*

Both the patriotic upsurge of 1914 and the nationalist frustration due to the Treaty of Versailles in 1919 excited the passion of many writers, and their writings in turn fanned the flames of the people. A climate ensued in which Hitler could rise. Even nationalists who had no love for Hitler contributed to this, only to be pushed aside once he was in the saddle. As has happened more than once in history, the intellectuals who had helped a totalitarian government to power were quickly eliminated: Ernst Niekisch and Othmar Spann were imprisoned and put on the rack; Edgar Jung was killed, while Ernst Jünger and Oswald Spengler, both too famous for liquidation, were quoted when it suited the bosses and silenced when it did not.

The intellectuals who took the road of nationalism thereby receded from the eternal postulates of their vocation; they saw and considered only part of the truth.

KLAUS MEHNERT

Their thought was concentrated on a small part of humanity—their nation or race—and in their demand for the nation's liberty they belittled, or completely denied, the liberty of the individual. The nation and the world paid dearly for this in the years of that very Third Reich so enthusiastically proclaimed by its prophets.

After this disastrous excursion into nationalism, the German intellectuals returned to the eternal ideals forsaken by so many of them. Today, the intellectual climate of Germany differs fundamentally from the one I grew up in after the First World War. In 1920, I was one of thousands of German children sent abroad by the Red Cross, half starved and sickly as a result of the wartime blockade of Germany. I spent four months with a family in northern Sweden. Two years ago, I revisited the little town for the first time in more than four decades. To refresh my memory, I took the package of letters I had written home from Sweden in 1920 and which, somehow, had survived the destructions of the Hitler era. I was astonished and appalled by the fierce nationalism that burned in those letters written by my thirteen-year-old self. The German Empire had gone down in defeat, my father had been killed in action on the Western Front, the Kaiser had fled, entire provinces had been lost—yet here I was with a little self-made black-white-red flag, the flag of the defunct Empire, trying to explain to the Swedes that German nationalism was still very much alive!

Nothing of this after the Second World War! Of course, there is, among those Germans who have lost everything in Eastern Europe, some yearning for a return to their homes; it would be surprising if this were not so. But the German intellectuals, with hardly an exception, do not give their minds or their pens to such movements, and so these do not have a wide echo in the country. The problem of the Eastern territories occupied by Poland is treated by the intellectuals as a political issue, not as an emotional one, and it is not one of their major preoccupations, as it would have been in the post-Versailles climate.

The question of unification is different; this is a highly emotional issue, but it seems to me more on humanitarian than nationalist grounds. It is a highly emotional issue mainly because the Germans in the West know that the Germans who live under Ulbricht's rule are, in the great majority, profoundly unhappy with life under an unwanted regime that must build walls and watchtowers along its borders to prevent its population from running away. The drive for unification in West Germany would become less passionate if the people across the wall were not forced to live under a regime which is still essentially Stalinist.

The West Berlin students who, at the risk of their lives and sometimes aided by students from other free countries, dig tunnels under the wall do this primarily to help people escape a hated environment, although, of course, the fact that these happen to be German brethren has something to do with it; however, the ready acceptance in Germany of tens of thousands of Hungarians who fled their country in 1956 showed that help is extended by no means only to German refugees from Communist rule.

The extent to which nationalism has faded in Germany can best be seen in the strong European tendencies among the German intellectuals who, like myself, advocate the formation of the United States of Europe of which they want Germany to become a part, willing to abandon the cherished prerogatives of a sovereign state.

The author most widely read in Germany and also abroad (including the Communist countries) is Heinrich Böll. In his writings, and most clearly in his three latest books, *Billiards at Half Past Nine, The Clown, Departure from the Troup,* Böll writes in a vein ages removed from the spirit of the nationalist writers of the period between the wars, of authors like Hans Grima, for example. Humanism is the dominating note in his melody. He praises what he calls the Sacrament of the Lamb as against the Sacrament of the Bull—that is, against force and violence. And the most successful German philosophers of our day are Karl Jaspers and Carl Friedrich von Weizsaecker; they are successful precisely because of their preoccupation with humanism and peace.

THE OTHER DEVIATION—MATERIALISM

The other deviation among German intellectuals was materialism, as distinct from utilitarianism, about which Sir Denis Brogan has written. Just as nationalism is an impoverishment of the world view, although, of course, the nations are facts and although tradition, sense for historical continuity, and bonds of language are values, so materialism is an impoverishment of the spirit, although, again of course, the *materia* is a fact and although the will for social advancement, the search for the understanding and utilization of nature are values.

Both nationalism and materialism mean a narrowing down of the great values, a limitation to and concentration on single aspects of life at the expense of others, the abandoning of the all-embracing totality of the intellectual pursuit. It was Germans such as Ludwig Andreas Feuerbach, Karl Marx, and Friedrich Engels who were responsible for the deviation of German thought to materialism, for the overemphasis of matter over spirit. But in Russia, rather than in Germany, this development reached its climax.

The intellectual history of nineteenth-century Russia has been studied with greater care in America than anywhere else. An entire bookshelf could be filled with American books on this subject; among them would be *The Russian Intelligentsia,* edited by R. Pipes, or G. Fisher's *Russian Liberalism from Gentry to Intelligentsia,* and there would be articles, too, such as Alan P. Pollard's "The Russian Intelligentsia: The Mind of Russia." The reader of these studies is made aware of the extraordinary continuity of Russian thought in the last two hundred years, though I myself may be more conscious of it than most because of my background. My parents, both German citizens born in Moscow, had grown up in the spirit of the Russian intelligentsia; my father was a painter and my mother, the daughter of a well-to-do family, followed in her youth the then-frequent Russian urge of "going to the people" by teaching children of poor Russian homes. At the outbreak of the First World War, we moved to Germany, and it was only in 1929 that, as a student, I saw Russia again.

From Pushkin to the writers of the 1920s, the great Russian writers and poets acted as the conscience of the nation, following the pursuit of truth, humanism, and liberty, often in strong—and sometimes dangerous—opposition to the regime. In their novels and poems they voiced the hopes, dreams and demands of the people.

Within the stream of Russian thought at that time there was one current which drew its inspiration from the German materialist school, with Nikolai Chernyshevsky as their leader. Although later the Bolsheviks were to proclaim all great Russian writers as their spiritual ancestors, it is only with regard to the materialists that this is really true. Even the other intellectual schools continued, however, after the victory of Lenin's revolution—that is, far into the twenties—although they encountered increasing difficulties in their work and quite a few of their members left the country, some to return later.

Only under Stalin did the deviation of Russian intellectuals from their true goals become complete. "Socialist Realism" was in fact nothing but the glorification of a tyrannical regime and of its day-by-day needs. Literature lost its autonomy, it became a tool of the dictator, its function was reduced to putting in rhymes the slogans of the Party. It is not much of an overstatement if I say that literature *per se* ceased to exist in Russia for, roughly, a quarter of a century—from about 1930 to 1954. Almost all that was of literary value was written before that time; even Mikhail Sholokhov, whom Stalin liked to claim as proof for the flourishing of the novel in his age, wrote the important portions of his *And Quiet Flows the Don* before this period.

What was written during the Stalinist era is of interest today only to the political historian, not to the student of literature. The same can be said about other arts—the theater, painting, and the films. One by one, the masters were silenced—or killed: Babel, Mandelshtam, Olesha, Pilnyak, Koltsov, Zamyatin, Meyerhold, Eisenstein, and many others. There remained opportunists, like Ehrenburg, or nonentities.

During the Second World War, as Professor Fainsod has said, there was a brief interruption of this dreary process. In addition to Simonow, whom he named, one might mention Alexander Chakovsky, whose novel about wartime Leningrad, *Eto bylo v Leningrade,* dealt exclusively with the human aspect of war, dispensing entirely with Party admonitions. But after the war was won, the censors again clamped down on the writers. Stalin obviously thought that he was sufficiently strong to override all hopes for intellectual leniency.

To be sure, the Party—and Stalin personally—never disassociated themselves from the ideals of Russian intellectuals. They claimed to have truth on their side, even naming their extremely one-sided daily *Pravda*; they frequently proclaimed their policy to be humanistic, preferring, however, to speak of Socialist Humanism. The Chinese have been bolder—and more honest—in this respect; humanism for the men around Mao is a depreciatory word, for, in being romantic about humanity as a whole, it blurs the clear lines of the class struggle. The Russian communists also maintain that liberty was one of their aims, and that, in fact, true liberty existed only in socialist countries. But none of these claims is to be taken too seriously. While paying lip service to the ideals, Stalin violated them daily in a thousand ways. This statement requires no proof; since 1956, the Russian communists themselves, led by Khrushchev, have admitted this openly time and again.

Professor Fainsod has spoken of what happened after Stalin's death; if I add a few words I do this not in disagreement with him but rather to strengthen his thesis. In connection with my line of argument, it is important to note that the contemporary Russian intellectuals returned as soon as possible to the public preoccupation with the ideals of their nineteenth-century precursors. To do this is still a dangerous thing but no longer as dangerous as in Stalin's day. One remembers the case of Boris Pasternak and the abuse heaped upon him in the Soviet Union after the publication of *Doctor Zhivago* abroad. He was called publicly a swine by Semichastney, now head of the police machinery of the Soviet Union.

Was there anything offensive to the Party in the book? Not at all; yet it was unacceptable to the Party bosses because of its exclusive concern with truth, humanity, and liberty. This point I had made in a lengthy review of the novel in a German weekly, a copy of which I sent to Pasternak. In an unsigned letter—he had learned by then to be cautious—written in his unmistakable, beautiful, almost Goethean script and in flawless German, he told me that he was in full agreement with my analysis. In particular, I had called the German reader's attention to one of the most revealing—and moving—scenes of the book. Lara, Zhivago's beloved, stands at his bier and in her thoughts she says to him (and I quote from memory), "You and I, we have known all the great things in life—nakedness, and love, and death. But as to the little things, such as the changing of the world—these have not been our concern." Truly, the perspective of a pure-bred intellectual, a complete reversal of the scale of values as compared with that of the Party! The declared aim of the Communists for which they were willing to sacrifice everything, the changing of the world—a little thing!

But Pasternak was an old man when this occurred, and it is perhaps not too surprising that a man whose roots reached to pre-Stalin, and even to pre-Lenin, days, thought and wrote the way he did in his great novel. It is far more important and surprising that the young generation of Russian writers thinks and writes in the same vein. Let me mention in proof of this a personal experience with one of the best known young Soviet poets to whom Professor Fainsod refers—Yevgeny Yevtushenko.

During one of his trips abroad, I spent a day with him at Munich. Among the persons he wanted to meet through me was Maria Schell, the film actress. Why her? I asked. Because he had seen one of her films which he liked very much and which he wanted to discuss with her. It was "The Last Bridge," a German-Yugoslav co-production about the war between the German army and the Yugoslav guerrillas during the Second World War. Maria Schell played the part of a German doctor attached to the Wehrmacht. The Yugoslavs capture her to make her treat their wounded and sick comrades. At first, she refuses to help the enemy, then she overcomes her national scruples and decides that it is a doctor's duty to care for the enemy, too. She is killed on a bridge crossing a ravine, the two sides of which are being held by the opposing forces. Thus, the bridge referred to in the title becomes a symbol for the overcoming of differences between hostile camps, and Maria Schell the symbol of a victim of that same great and noble task. Yevtushensko's conversation with Maria Schell, which I interpreted, turned largely around the artist's mediating role in a world of opposing camps.

Later that evening, the question about the individual and the collective arose. What did he, Yevtushenko was asked, think about it—he the citizen of a collectivist country? The poet answered by reciting some of his verses. Freely translated, they began with the stanzas:

> Uninteresting people don't exist
> for all of us are interesting
> in his or her own way . . . .

The poet compared each human being with a planet, a world in itself, unique, irreproducible, and full of mysteries. Is there, I ask, in any country of individualist creed a poet who has sung higher praise to the individual than this young man from Siberia who had spent his whole life in a country with a collectivist dogma?

It was out of respect for truth, for the rights of the human being and his liberty, when Yevtushenko defended his friend, the modernist sculptor Neizvestny, against Khrushchev's attacks during an artists' meeting in Moscow. When Khrushchev continued to abuse the sculptor, saying that he seemed in his work as unnatural as a hunchback and quoting ominously the Russian saying "The grave will heal the hunchbacks," it took courage for Yevtushenko to say: "We hope, Nikita Sergeyevitch, you did not mean to say that we are going back to an era where decisions were enforced by means of the grave."

Even so, one might say, poets are poets! How about others among the intelligentsia, the engineers, for example? Perhaps Yevtushenko and his like are freaks, outsiders in Soviet Society, lone wolves which can be found at all times? On the contrary! Several times when he recited his poems Yevtushenko had to hire the Moscow Stadium. His is not a solitary voice; he speaks for a large part of the new Russian intelligentsia which see in him and other writers of his type their avant garde and which rejoice when the poets and poetesses of Russia express their feelings and outlook on life.

Some time ago, a Russian visited me in my home. I did not know him, but he had heard that I was interested in his country and that I spoke his language. He was an engineer, in his late thirties, who had attended one of the German technological fairs and was about to return to his homeland. "What is on your mind?" I asked him after we had settled down.

"Well," he said, "I have a whole lot of questions. But I shall start with the most important one—what is the meaning of life?"

I showed my surprise. "You, a Russian communist, ask *me* about the meaning of life? Have you not been told by your teachers, youth leaders, Komosomol and Party lecturers ever since you can remember what—according to the Communist view—life's meaning is?"

"Of course," he shrugged, "all that I know by heart. But I want to know the *real* meaning of life."

The Russian intellectuals have also rediscovered conscience, which, under Stalin, had disappeared from sight. The truth was all his—or the Party's. If your conscience told you differently, you'd better discard it and chase it into the farthest corner of your brain, out of harm's way. But now the Russians find out that Stalin was wrong and their conscience was right all along! After the fall of Khrushchev, they are being told that he, too, was wrong and again their conscience was right! Then the conscience is a more reliable guide in life than the Party? Every new Soviet novel about Stalin's concentration camps in Siberia enforces the doubts about the Party's wisdom and strengthens the case for the superiority of one's conscience.

The intellectuals' duty, I have stated, is to study the currents of their time, to understand and finally even to influence them—to be the weather makers of their tribe, of mankind. This, it seems to me, is exactly what the Soviet intellectuals are doing. They affect the climate in which their chieftains then rule. I do not overestimate their power, but I think their influence is steadily growing. Without years of patient attacks on the part of the intellectually leading Soviet lawyers, Stalin's penal code would not have been changed, in 1958, into a more humane one. Without years of patient effort on the part of the intellectually leading economists, Soviet industrial management would still be in the rut of yesterday's heavy-handed planning system. Soviet sociology only came into existence some years ago because the intellectuals who had attended international sociological conferences were ashamed of what their country had to contribute to this field. Soviet scientists are allowed to read foreign journals because for many years they have been pointing out that without them they would not be able to compete with the West. The rehabilitation of Albert Einstein, the fall of Stalin's court biologist, Lyssenko, for a long time the scourge of countless Soviet scientists—these are all results of the concerted and patient labors of Soviet intellectuals.

There are, of course, fields in which the Russian intellectuals cannot do anything—at least not yet. The study of modern history, for example, which the Party leaders consider an extremely sensitive area, they prefer to manipulate all by themselves. Even more is this the case with the truly political fields, although the changing of the penal code comes pretty close to the political nerve system. But already, the intellectuals have contributed greatly to the change of the climate in which the Party operates.

In a way, one might say that the present Soviet intellectuals—as those of the nineteenth century—are taking the place of the nonexistent parliament. In their novels and plays, in their poems and stories, they express what, in other countries, might be said from the rostrum of the nation's representation. It is probably with this in mind that one of the most popular young poets, Bulat Okudjava, has written a popular song which begins—and ends—with the line, addressed to the Soviet people:

Take care of us, the poets, take care of us!

INTELLECTUAL AND STATE

One word must be said about the relationship between the intellectuals and the state. This relationship depends, of course, on the character of the state. One which is authoritarian, even totalitarian, is a natural enemy of the intellectual, of the man who tries to think for himself, who refuses to swallow the "party line," who demands the right to criticize. In a state of this kind, it is not without danger to have an independent mind, to be a weather maker. In Hermann Hesse's story, incidentally, the weather maker is killed, in the end, by the tribe. There is a long list of attacks by totalitarian governments against the intellectuals, the most famous one having been performed by Emperor Shih Huang-ti of China in the third century A.D., who ordered the intellectuals killed and their books burned.

The intellectual is more welcome in democratic states that have open societies, but only up to a point, as the misgivings about "eggheads" in America show. It is all to the good if there exists a certain amount of tension between the intellectuals and the state, provided that the intellectual is true to his vocation and the state is serving the interests of the people. In totalitarian states, people develop a kind of "sixth sense" for registering and understanding the "signals" of the intellectuals; they have learned how "to read not the black but the white"—*i.e.* between the lines. More than that: they are eager to get hold of ideas which have not even found a "black" frame, which have not yet been printed. In a recent copy of a Soviet literary journal, this quest for the unprinted is described:

"Don't talk to me about literature! If there is a person who knows contemporary literature, it is me. Journals? Periodicals? That's all nonsense! What they print officially, I don't even read. What good would it do? My friends obtain literature for me in the form of typewritten notebooks. Those are truly creations, full of glamor! . . . And not only notebooks . . . . Sometimes they put such poems on tapes!"

To avoid a misunderstanding, it should be noted that I am not against *littérature engagée,* against writers' taking a position in political issues. But even a *littérature engagée* is still literature, not political action. Of course, the intellectuals should be interested in politics, they should study its forces and currents, they should report about their findings, and they should influence the course of events—with the aid of their medium, which is thought and word, not deed.

THE THIRD WORLD

There is one more area that deserves attention—that of the developing countries, the Third World. In these countries which lack a larger middle class, the intellectuals are of particular importance. Their attitude is, because of the similarity of their situation to that of underdeveloped Russia in the nineteenth century, in some respects like the position of the Russian intelligentsia during that period. As were the Russians then, they are divided today into a Westernized group which looks for the solution of the country's problems in the political and economic systems of the West and in a nationalist wing which hates the superior West to the point of almost self-destruction. Whichever wing they belong to, they have been largely responsible for the orientation of their peoples, and some of them have, due to the lack of political leaders in their country, entered the political arena. Frequently, they have done this not very enthusiastically, and often also without success. U Nu is one of them, an intellectual if there ever was one, with the emphasis on truth-seeking and humanism—who is being held in prison by his unintellectual, but stronger, rival.

In these countries, intellectuals have often felt like having been "drafted" into politics because there was—apart from the generals or colonels—nobody available to do this job. It was a draft of another kind which led German intellectuals like Eugen Gerstenmaier or Adolf Rechwein into active political participation, although they had wished for nothing better than intellectual pursuit. More than that: they entered into a deadly dangerous conspiracy for the assassination of Hitler, the twentieth of July, 1944, plot.* They had felt "drafted" for the same reason: under the prevailing conditions of wartime, in Hitler's Germany there were very few available for this task.

Let us summarize my thesis: apart from exceptions and from exceptional conditions, intellectuals, as defined above, should stay out of active politics, also defined above. Their noble task—not less important, but surely also not more important, than that of the statesman—lies in their indirect influence on the political destiny of their country and of the world. In this, they form a worldwide brotherhood. All men in pursuit of wisdom are brethren under heaven, as one of the ancient Chinese sayings has it. In this spirit, I say: for truth, humanism, and liberty—intellectuals of the world, unite!

* A good account of this movement, including the position of the intellectuals, can be found in *Germany against Hitler* (by Terrence Prittie). London, 1964.

KLAUS MEHNERT

JOHN BRADEMAS : *The Role of the Intellectual in Politics—*
An American View

FIFTEEN YEARS AGO I WAS ONE OF THIRTY-TWO AMERICAN RHODES SCHOLARS
arriving in Oxford and the only one who had decided on a career in electoral
politics. Ten years later, however, back at Oxford for some lectures, I was be-
sieged by American students seeking advice on how to run for Congress. In 1954,

when I first ran (unsuccessfully) for Congress, my chief mentor, Paul M. Butler, who later became Chairman of the Democratic National Committee, warned me not to publicize unduly my Harvard-Oxford background during my campaign in Indiana, although it was largely this that had caused him to support me; yet, four years later, after the Soviet Sputnik had jarred Americans into a sudden willingness to spend more money on education, my local political leaders were urging citizens of the Third Indiana District to "vote for Brademas because he has a fine education."

A recent series of interviews by a Washington journalist with Congressmen and Senators suggests that Congressional politics is now attracting an increasing number of younger men whose university education would, in earlier years, have led them into academic or other professional careers, but certainly not into what Adlai Stevenson used to call "combat politics." The reasons the Congressmen assigned for this trend—it is not yet possible to say how deep or lasting it is—are several. The electorate itself is much better educated and is increasingly willing to support education, as the remarkable success of education legislation in the 88th and present Congresses attests; so education must be all right in politicians, too! President Kennedy's administration, moreover, brought a new respect for the intellectual and cultural community generally which was in sharp contrast to the White House attitude during the Eisenhower years. Now, even the younger Republicans in Congress bewail their lack of support in the academic community and are seeking ways to win it!

I shall focus upon American politics, particularly upon the intellectual as a politician, and, because it is the scene I know best, the politician elected to Congress.

The first problem, of course, is: what do we mean by an intellectual? The way we define "intellectual" may be decisive in trying to understand his role as a politician. President Eisenhower, speaking at Los Angeles in 1954, said an intellectual was "a person who takes more words than necessary to say more than he knows." While this is, in at least one respect, revealing, it is not the most useful definition for our purposes. Some writers define intellectuals functionally, describing them in terms of what they do rather than how they do it. Yet there is, as Richard Hofstadter suggests, a distinction between "intelligence" and "intellect" which is even more relevant to our understanding of the intellectual's role in politics:

". . . Intelligence is an excellence of mind that is employed within a fairly narrow, immediate and predictable range; it is a manipulative, adjustive, unfailingly practical quality. . . . Intelligence works within the framework of limited but clearly stated goals. . . .

". . . Intellect, on the other hand, is a critical, creative, and contemplative side of mind. Whereas intelligence seeks to grasp, manipulate, re-order, adjust, intellect examines, ponders, wonders, theorizes, criticizes, imagines. Intelligence will see the immediate meaning in a situation and evaluate it. Intellect evaluates evaluations, and looks for the meanings of situations as a whole. . . ."

The stress on inner attitudes rather than particular vocations, on the critical rather

JOHN BRADEMAS

than the adjustive faculty, on the total situation rather than limited goals, on the capacity to see the relationships among seemingly unrelated facts—these distinguish the intellectual from the intelligent man. The distinction is, of course, descriptive rather than moral.

If we accept Hofstadter's differentiation between intelligence and intellect, we must, I think, conclude that in political life we need both men of intelligence and men of intellect; for in politics, as in every other field, we must have "intelligent" men who are capable of operating "within the framework of limited but clearly stated goals." But just as we need "intelligent" men in politics, in both the executive and legislative branches, we also need some "intellectual" men. That is to say, we need persons who are willing to evaluate the evaluations, to raise questions about the policies themselves as well as the methods for implementing policies, willing, indeed, to inquire into the presuppositions on the basis of which policies are made.

Politics—even electoral politics—requires more than first-class technicians, indispensable as these are. If our society is to remain open and free, if it is not to stumble and falter when confronted with the enormous problems we face, there must be in decision-making positions in our government—in Congress—and not only as advisors but as principals, at least some men who are deeply concerned with objectives and assumptions as well as with techniques and methods. There must be some men who are interested in rethinking policy as well as explaining it, interested not only in making present policies work, but in asking whether they are right. There must be at least some politicians who do not feel, in David Reisman's phrase, "threatened with complexity," but challenged and stimulated by it.

My thesis is only in part exaggerated by the words of the nineteenth-century political reporter and war correspondent who was also briefly Librarian of the House of Representatives and Minister to France, Whitelaw Reid. He said, in a speech at Dartmouth in 1873, "We may set it down as, within certain needful and obvious limitations, the very foremost function of the scholar in politics, *to oppose the established*." To view the status quo critically and not simply to be its servant is, I believe, the appropriate role of the intellectual in politics as well as out of it. He may finally decide—or he may not—to attack established policy; as an intellectual, however, his chief vocation is to scrutinize it.

It is not difficult to understand how intellectuals outside politics can carry on, more or less effectively, this kind of searching, critical enterprise. The central question for our purposes here, however, is the extent to which it is possible for the "intellectual" man to be part of the process of politics itself, to help run the country, as it were, and still raise probing questions about what the government is doing, to be both a politician and an intellectual.

We must be careful not to make our distinctions too arbitrary. The really critical question may be put by politicians who do not pretend to be "intellectual." So much the worse for those who should be asking questions!

One useful way of understanding the role of intellectuals in politics in the United

States is to consider their sharply contrasting situation in Latin America. First, the definition of "intellectual" there is much broader: even the university students, as well as graduates, regard themselves as intellectuals and are so regarded by society. This has certainly not been the case in the United States, where students, although they have in recent years displayed an increasing interest in political issues, especially civil rights and peace, have not evidenced a comparable commitment to activity within the political parties. The student movement at Berkeley is no sure breeding ground of congressmen and senators. Protest is not politics.

Latin-American intellectuals are preoccupied with a complete overhaul of society. They are, as John P. Harrison of the University of Texas, has noted

". . . more concerned with the re-structuring of society than in finding solutions to the immediate and localized problems of economic and social development which concern their national governments. They are, in a very real sense, still fighting the *ancien régime*—something the intellectual of the left in the United States has never had to do. Their opposition is negative. The intellectuals constitute groups of individuals who refuse in principle to consider the problems of government as real tasks needing resolution."

Now I have said that the intellectual is, or at least ought to be, characterized by his disposition to think critically, by his willingness to question the status quo; yet, unlike the Latin Americans, as Reisman complains, "the great majority of intellectuals [in the United States] . . . have only peripheral political interests. They do not conceive of their role in society as implying an obligation to warn that society of impending danger. . . ." Even the North American intellectual who is not apolitical but engages in politics sounds less critical of society than his Latin-American counterpart. The reason is succinctly advanced by de Tocqueville: "The great advantage of the [North] American is that he has arrived at a state of democracy without having to endure a democratic revolution; and that he is born free without having to become so."

An example that points up the difference between the United States and the rest of the world in this respect is to be found, I think, in a recent address by a son of Texas, Lyndon B. Johnson, in his civil rights address, in which he proclaimed to Congress and the nation, "We shall overcome," and called upon the American people to make real the promise of the Declaration of Independence and the Constitution. The point is that, though some Americans oppose the *reality*, almost nobody quarrels with the *promise*, with what Gunnar Myrdal has called "the American dream." Myrdal's penetrating conclusion must be recalled: "America is . . . conservative . . . but the principles conserved are liberal and some, indeed, are radical." Also to be recalled in this context is President Johnson's speech in March 1965, in which he urged Congressional action on a voting-rights bill:

"This was the first nation in the history of the world to be founded with a purpose. The great phrases of that purpose still sound in every American heart, North and South: 'All men are created equal'—'government by consent of the governed'—'give me liberty or give me death.' Those are not just clever words. Those are not just empty theories. . . ."

I offer these observations because, having suggested that an essential responsibility of the intellectual in politics is to consider things as they are with a critical eye, I must add that the vocabulary of criticism in a society born free is likely to sound less shattering, the rhetoric less revolutionary, than in Europe or Latin America. Yet the impact of words long traditional in America may be revolutionary still, as Governor Wallace is learning from President Johnson's speech and from Martin Luther King's sermons. The mass registration of Negro voters in Alabama will mean change, not immediately, of course, but in time, and no little change.

The point to be made here is that American intellectuals—and this is directly relevant to their role in politics—operate from a different base from intellectuals in less open societies, societies with feudal walls still to be stormed. This means their criticisms here are less likely to be aimed at social institutions themselves (though perhaps in some cases they should be) and more at improving or modernizing existing institutions. Working from an accepted liberal base, they can, in fact, be more conservative. Everybody agrees that the Negro has the right to vote. The flame and fury are therefore directed to the problem of *how* we can be sure he does vote. Indispensable mechanics, no doubt, but mechanics all the same, for the goal is settled. As the President said, "There is no constitutional issue here . . . there is no moral issue. . . ."

To cite another example: everybody—well nearly everybody—agrees, at least publicly, that widespread poverty in a wealthy land is wrong, so there is little dispute about the purpose of the war on poverty. Almost all the quarrels are about how to wage the war. Who gets the federal money—public or private agencies? How much should the poor themselves have to say about the program? And who really speaks for the poor?

What all this means is that American intellectuals will often seem to be giving their attention to means rather than ends, but as I have already indicated, in a society in which the principle of universal suffrage is still not universally practiced, preoccupation with methods can be just as revolutionary as bold declarations of purpose.

Even so circumscribed, the mission of the intellectual as politician is difficult. There may be some justification for Richard Neustadt's contention, "The politics of well-established government has rarely been attractive to and has rarely dealt kindly with the men whom intellectuals regard as first-rate intellects."

It is pertinent to discuss some of the difficulties encountered by intellectuals, defined as I have defined them, who become active politicians, especially elected ones—senators and representatives.

It is banal but no less true to say that one of the great enemies of the politician is time. For the modern congressman, this is particularly true; he is expected to be not one man, but many men; ambassador from his district to Washington that he may bring back good things to the people he represents, in the form of defense contracts, highway funds, science installations, and, now, even anti-poverty projects; he must be a lawyer for his constituents in their dealings with the executive agencies affecting veterans and social security pensioners, post offices, and military academy appointments; he must be a politician, for his survival depends on his relations with the voters and political leaders in his state; on occasion, he must be an educator, explaining issues to his electorate; he is also, if time remains, a legislator. The list could be lengthened. But so time- and energy-consuming has become the combination of these several roles that the conscientious representative or senator is hard-pressed to keep up with them, let alone to read the books and engage in the dialogues that are the daily diet of the practicing intellectual. Senator Gale McGee, of Wyoming, in a moment of desperation, has even suggested that Congressmen should be required to take sabbatical leaves for reading and reflection on the issues on which they vote. His is a noble if utopian thought!

Inadequate staffing is symbolic of another burden Congress imposes upon itself, a burden which seriously impairs its capacity to cope critically and imaginatively with complicated issues. Members of Congress vote vast sums for science, for example, often without much comprehension of the implications of the expenditures. This is not to say that congressmen should try to become scientists, though perhaps we could use at least a few; it is to say that Congress is utterly outmanned by the executive branch in quantity, if not quality, of expert advice. Politicians who have a genuine desire to understand the big issues are thereby seriously handicapped. As Hubert Humphrey once said, "The balance between the legislative and executive branches can never be righted until the legislature has within its mechanism the kind of brains that the executive departments have long been able to attract."

A third and related problem that thoughtful representatives and senators soon encounter is that wars and depressions and the welfare state have given the executive—the President, specifically—a monopoly of initiative in the legislative process. Coupled with the conservative bias built into the machinery of Congress—the seniority system is the most obvious example—this loss of initiative makes it most difficult for a legislator to play the role assigned him, that of, as one perceptive observer put it, "a national prophet, a civic risktaker as well as preserver." The congressman is more equipped in these circumstances to concentrate on the narrower, safer needs of individuals and groups in his district and to neglect the larger, more complex problems of the nation.

Hans Morgenthau warns that if an intellectual in government surrenders his proper role, "which is to think for the sake of thinking . . ." he "becomes at best a practitioner and at worst an ideologue of social action. Thus the intellectual ceases to be the conscience of society and becomes its agent." We have seen, especially in Nazi Germany and in the Soviet Union, what happens when the intellectual becomes an ideologue and so perverts his calling; but even in a free society, the intel-

JOHN BRADEMAS

lectual may allow himself to be used simply as an apologist for the status quo.

I discussed this paper with Paul Goodman, one of the most radical critics of American society, who warned me of the seductions of what he called "tokenism." By this he meant that even the thoughtful politician may settle for a policy which is, in fact, only a surface attack on a given problem and fails to get at its roots. Goodman cited the war on poverty as an example. I think he is only half right, but there is disturbing truth in his admonition. In like fashion, the intellectual can serve government as a technician only, helping to make an existing policy work rather than considering whether the policy itself is right. As Marcus Raskin puts it:

"There is no great difference between someone who has a Ph.D. and works at a particular problem [for the government] and the skilled or unskilled workers supported by a particular industry. For purposes of economic and political analysis, they play essentially the same role.

"In the government, a person is given the frame of reference in which he is to think about the problem. The task for the intellectual in this context is managerial or administrative, rather than moral or political. It is not 'fundamental'. . . ."

President Truman in effect endorsed this view a few years ago in replying to a question about intellectuals in government. "I think intellectuals in government are great," he said, "as long as there's an old pro to tell them what to do."

Once in politics, the intellectual will probably not feel as free to criticize as he felt in private life, for he is now, by virtue of his office, responsible for his actions. I use "responsible" in the sense that what an elected public official says and how he votes are likely, though, of course, not necessarily, to have more direct influence on others in or out of government than do the views of a private citizen. The greater the degree of his responsibility in Congress the more inhibited may be the politician's freedom to criticize. It is one thing for junior senators to attack U.S. policy in South Viet Nam, but, assuming (as many in Washington do assume) that Senators Mansfield and Fulbright share these misgivings, it is a far different matter, and more difficult, for the Majority Leader of the Senate and the chairman of the Foreign Relations Committee to voice such thoughts. They may genuinely feel that for them to do so is to give aid and comfort to the enemy. The ambition to achieve greater influence with his colleagues—neither an illegal nor wholly unadmirable attribute of most congressmen—may become a further check on the instinct to criticize on the part of the intellectual who gets himself elected. "If you want to get along, go along," Sam Rayburn used to counsel freshman Congressmen seeking to learn the ways of the House and how to advance within it.

The organization and folkways of the House and Senate are not designed to encourage dissent; indeed, suspicion quickly adheres to the congressman who talks too critically too often on the floor of the House, especially if the offender covers too wide a range of subjects. These suspicions are not always without justification. In fact, some observers divide the liberals in the House of Representatives into two groups: the "bomb throwers" and the less vocal but usually more effective "operators." I have observed in a number of instances that the greater the degree of political security a congressman develops back home, the more willing he is to assume positions in Washington that are probably not too popular in his constituency. There is, of course, a corollary danger which comes with such security: increased seniority and enhanced power may make the congressman less willing to rock the boat of the Congressional establishment with sharply divergent views.

When a strong President is in the White House, members of his own party in Congress must not assume he is entirely unmindful of their votes on closely contested key issues or unwilling to remember them, as many can testify from experience. For example, months after I had voted against the Administration position on the closely contested cotton-wheat bill in early 1964, President Johnson reminded me of my vote and then chided me further by saying how pleased he was to see that a firm in my district had that week received a large defense contract!

Another obvious—and salutary—counterpoise for the man with a propensity to think critically is his obligation to represent his constituency. It is true that senators and representatives depend for their continuance in office on the voters of their districts; yet politicians give great weight to the views of the citizens they represent not only because of a desire for reëlection but because this is the way democracy operates.

Just as the intellectual in politics, if he pretends to be true to his vocation as an intellectual, has an obligation to think critically, he has also at least some responsibility, as a politician, to try to survive in political office. He does not, normally, deliberately choose to lose the election; this explains why someone—I think it was Grover Cleveland—once said, "The doctrine of vicarious atonement does not apply to politics."

Certainly, no one should be surprised to hear senators remarking that the six-year term they enjoy gives them a feeling of far greater freedom to speak out on controversial issues than when they served in the House and felt themselves constantly under the gun of the two-year term. There is even now talk of a Constitutional amendment to extend the House term to four years.

To be able to vote more freely in the national interest as they see it, some members of Congress work with great diligence to build independent political strength in their districts by effectively tending to constituents' requests and by bringing home the many kinds of federal bacon. President Kennedy told the American Foreign Service Association, in 1962, "Every Member of Congress who subjects you to abuse is being subjected himself, every two years, to the possibility that his career also will come to an end. He doesn't live a charmed life. You have to remember that the hot breath is on him also. . . ."

I trust that I shall not here be accused of arguing that a politician's chief duty is victory at the polls and that he must therefore seek at all costs to win. On the contrary, if a politician takes his calling seriously, he must always be prepared for defeat on certain controversial issues about which he has deep convictions; but there is a time for living and a time for dying, and the politician who leaps to his white horse to lead every crusade which is pressed upon him will find both himself and his mount wearied before long. Because intellectuals are likely, in the nature of things, to have a variety of interests, they are also more likely to take on more causes than they can effectively champion. Representative Richard Bolling in his new book *House Out of Order* is particularly caustic with some of his fellow liberals for spreading themselves too thin over a number of issues, thereby diluting their capacity to affect any.

One of the most difficult problems for some intellectuals outside politics to appreciate is the nature of the political process itself. That process is one in which accommodation, negotiation, and compromise are the words characteristically and accurately used to describe what happens when, not to mention all the other actors in the drama, four hundred and thirty-five representatives and one hundred senators work with or against one President. Accommodation, negotiation, and compromise are all non-normative words. But they are not the words customarily used to describe the mission of the intellectual as I have defined him. Perhaps that is why the twentieth-century British civil servant and writer Sir Henry Taylor, in his classic little volume *The Statesman,* could say: "The independent thinking of persons who have trained and habituated themselves to philosophical freedom of opinion is . . . unfavorable to statesmanship because the business of a statesman is less with truth at large than with truths commonly received."

The danger to the intellectual, then, is that he may disdain a process in which advance and achievement are usually the product of give and take rather than of discovery of "truth at large." The intellectual who becomes a member of Congress must remember that he is just that, not a member of a debating society. He is a member of a legislative body with business to do, not simply opinions to voice.

These are all problems that beset the intellectual man in elective politics, and they are troubling, for it is clearly in the national interest that at least some decision-makers in Washington—in Congress as well as in the executive branch—should be thinking in a most searching and critical way about the great issues that face our country and the world. President Kennedy used to say that a member of Congress early in the nineteenth century needed to be informed upon only three public problems: internal improvements, the tariff, and slavery. If a man came to Congress in the early 1800s and served twenty or thirty years, he would have few important matters to pass on other than these, and what he learned about each in his first years served him for the rest of his Congressional career. The life of a modern legislator is not as simple as in the days of Webster and Calhoun. This year alone the Congress will have acted on medicare, poverty, elementary and secondary education, right-to-work laws, voting rights, farm and foreign aid bills, housing, and defense, to cite only major legislative issues.

Whether or not we elect more intellectuals to Congress, it is clearly imperative that we maintain a flow of ideas between the politicians in Washington and the intellectual community throughout the nation. Walter Lippmann, in a recent television interview, paid effective tribute to the influence of ideas and of intellectuals on politics in the United States saying, "The great mistake of the Republican Party since the time of Theodore Roosevelt is that it quarreled with the intellectual community in the United States and alienated them, and then McCarthy's regime persecuted them, and they all went over to the Democrats and that gave the Democrats an intellectual capacity for dealing with issues that the Republicans simply didn't have."

The problem of assuring a continuing dialogue between the politicians and the intellectuals merits discussion. This is, for some of the reasons I have already set forth, a much more difficult enterprise for Congress than it is for the executive branch. The executive agencies such as the Defense Department, the National Aeronautics and Space Administration, the Atomic Energy Commission, and the National Institutes of Health—the most obvious users of scientific knowledge—have direct links with both university-based thinkers and people at the Rand-type institutes and the great foundations. It is, moreover, much easier for intellectuals to commute from the university or institute to the executive branch and back—witness Jerome Wiesner and James Killian, science advisors to the President, or any one of Sargent Shriver's Peace Corps and poverty-program administrators, or Harvard's contributions, John Kenneth Galbraith, Carl Kaysen, Seymour Harris—than it is for scholars and professors or other kinds of intellectuals to get elected to Congress and then, if defeated, to return to their previous positions.

It is significant that during nearly every recent campaign, the candidates for the Presidency have organized brain trust operations to supply themselves with position papers on major issues. For a year (1955–1956), I was in charge of research on issues for Adlai E. Stevenson's campaign, leaving after the August convention to return to Indiana and my own campaign for Congress. On several occasions during that year, I helped arrange discussion meetings in Chicago between Governor Stevenson and leading thinkers, and I was also in touch with a number of intellectuals both in and out of the university community by telephone, letter, or personal visit. I served as a kind of right arm to Thomas K. Finletter, recent ambassador to NATO, who coordinated Governor Stevenson's brain trust group. My job was to obtain ideas, memoranda, and position papers from such persons as Seymour Harris, Galbraith, and Alvin Hansen at Harvard, Walter Heller at Minnesota, Walter Johnson at Chicago, Paul Samuelson and E. Cary Brown at the Massachusetts Institute of Technology, Richard Musgrave, then at Michigan, and Joseph Rauh and Gerhard Colm in Washington. Many of these same persons provided John F. Kennedy with ideas in the 1960 campaign. Both Stevenson and Kennedy stimulated the intellectual community in this country as no Presidential politicians have done since Franklin D. Roosevelt in our own day and Woodrow Wilson over a generation ago.

JOHN BRADEMAS

Of Stevenson, in particular, I think it important to note that he elevated the politics of the Republic in two significant ways. He insisted that a candidate had the obligation to discuss the most serious issues facing the country, no matter how controversial they were or what effect they had on his candidacy. Stevenson suffered at the polls from his 1956 call for a nuclear test-ban treaty, but his courageous initiative bore fruit for Kennedy in 1963. Whereas Senator Dirksen says that a politician's responsibility is to recognize an idea whose time has come, as with civil rights, Stevenson insisted that the highest mission of a politician is to recognize the significance of the idea whose time has not yet come and to try to hasten the day. Secondly, Stevenson had a profound concern for the quality of American politics and politicians. "He gave us all a little class," I once heard Hubert Humphrey say. Adlai Stevenson made Kennedy possible and, in my judgment, more than most people realize he prepared the way for Lyndon Johnson's Great Society.

By citing the kind of tie that binds intellectuals to Presidential nominees and to the executive branch, I hope to point up the tenuousness of the relationship between the intellectual community and Congress. If intellectuals and their ideas are indispensable to the legislative as well as the executive branch, we must ask what we can do to improve the relationship between the scholars and the legislators.

First, we can try to stimulate more dialogue between Congress and the intellectual. More is going on in Washington in this respect right now than many realize. For example, the Brookings Institution, an independent organization of first-class researchers in the social sciences, has sponsored seminars for members of Congress at which some of the leading scientists in the nation have discussed the latest developments in astronomy, laser rays, population control, teaching machines, and oceanography. The Institute for Policy Studies, which began operations in Washington in 1963, was established precisely to enable scholars and government officials to "exchange ideas and collaborate on some of the problems most critically in need of new thought." The IPS carries on research and conducts seminars in such fields as education, civil rights, disarmament, and national security, foreign policy, the administration of criminal justice, the Alliance for Progress, and the anti-poverty program. In nearly all these enterprises, the Institute brings together scholars, labor leaders, members of Congress, and officials of the executive branch, in addition to its own researchers.

The latest effort to bridge the gap between the scholar and the politician is the Institute of Politics, to be established in connection with the Kennedy Memorial Library at Harvard. Richard E. Neustadt, advisor to both Presidents Truman and Kennedy, will be the director, and he plans to use the Institute to help meet the needs of elected as well as appointed government officials.

Late in 1963, Hubert Humphrey proposed the creation of a new arm of Congress—he called it a "Congressional Institute"—a group of scholars, selected by their peers, who would serve Congress as a "pool of knowledge, thought and expertise." Such a group could help Congress think ahead about some of the problems we all know will be with us in the coming decade: the Atlantic Alliance, population growth, tax policy, federal-state relations, international peace-keeping machinery. These scholars, serving for from one to three years, could rotate in Washington from our best universities and thereby encourage a flow of ideas both in Congress and in the university community.

Although the capacity of Congress to initiate legislation may be declining, Congress is more and more asserting its power to oversee the administration of programs it has enacted. Appalachia, the war on poverty, medicare, and elementary and secondary education programs—all will undoubtedly and quite properly bring new opportunities for Congress to inquire, study, and investigate. Congress will therefore need more expert advice, not less.

I am certain there are many other ways of improving the exchange of ideas between the political and intellectual communities. The final one, of course, is for more thoughtful, well-educated men and women to become candidates for Congress; more citizens of intellect and intelligence to become politicians.

I realize that the chief barrier to more direct participation by intellectuals in political life is their fear of the "compromise" it entails; however, I repeat that they mistakenly use the word morally rather than descriptively.

The world of the politician is, in many ways, different from that of the intellectual. Its style is not the same, the rewards are not the same, the objectives are not always the same. Where the intellectual seeks precision and clarity, the politician, charged with different responsibilities, may deliberately becloud an issue to assure himself the flexibility needed to reconcile conflicting interests. There may be at times a higher degree of morality in the calculated ambiguity of political utterance than the cynic is willing to admit.

In any event, the intellectual should be the first to understand the admonition of Bernard Crick in his book *In Defense of Politics:*

"To renounce or destroy politics is to destroy the very thing which gives order to the pluralism and variety of civilized society, the thing which enables us to enjoy variety without suffering either anarchy or the tyranny of single truths. . . ."

I believe, then, that a career in politics should, for several reasons, have increasing appeal to intelligent young men and women. There is a satisfaction in being involved, even with but one voice and vote, in decisions that shape the future of the country and the world. There is attraction, in an age of specialization, in a life that touches, even if tangentially, on a wide range of subjects—from unemployment to civil rights to foreign policy.

Finally, young men and women with convictions about the direction in which their country should move will find in Congress an opportunity to assert those convictions and thereby serve the republic. President Kennedy often quoted a Greek definition of happiness: "The exercise of vital powers along lines of excellence in a life affording them scope."

EUGENE J. MCCARTHY : *The Intellectual's Place in American Government*

ASUPERFICIAL READING OF THE POLITICAL HISTORY OF THE UNITED STATES supports the view that American politics is anti-intellectual and that American government—and its institutions—is a product of the efforts of "practical" men. Certainly, the Founding Fathers were "practical" men. Arnold Toynbee, in an address at Williamsburg, Virginia, in 1961, observed quite properly that: "Those great men were, of course, all agreed in working together for one objective that was immediate and definite. They were working for complete self-government for the thirteen colonies; and this political claim of theirs was based on precedent. They were claiming for themselves the political rights that the people of England had successfully asserted in the course of the preceding century, first in the English Civil War and then in the Revolution of 1688." They were taking practical political action, knowing that the consequences of failure were almost certainly to be realized in their execution as traitors.

At the same time, American politics is idealistic, and the reported division between politics and idealism is much more fancied than real. The failure to associate politics and politicians with the philosophical and intellectual arena of ideas arises, in part, from the very absence of genuine ideological conflict between men of ideas and men of action in American political life. Philosophers, historians, and men of ideas have been accepted as associates and advisers of politicians from the earliest days of our history.

G. K. Chesterton, in his book *What I Saw in America,* written in 1922, said, "America is the only nation in the world that is founded on a creed. That creed is set forth with dogmatic lucidity in the Declaration of Independence; perhaps the only piece of practical politics which is also theoretical politics and also great literature." The "creed" was expressed in the Declaration in these words: ". . . all men are created equal, . . . they are endowed by their Creator with certain inalienable rights, . . . among these are Life, Liberty and the pursuit of happiness. . . . ." These words and these ideas were taken seriously by the men who drafted the Declaration of Independence. They were spoken by men in danger of being shot or hanged if the revolution they led turned out to be a failure. The words and ideas they expressed were taken literally. They were not stated merely as a justification for the Revolution but were intended to establish a foundation in principle upon which democratic institutions and traditions could be established anywhere in the world. What was incorporated in these early documents was a product of the whole tradition of Western political thought from Plato to the humanist and rationalist philosophers of the eighteenth century.

The influence of ideas and of men of ideas in politics today is somewhat different from what it was 180 years ago—or a hundred years ago, or even forty years ago when Chesterton wrote that every time the world was in trouble the demand went up for a practical man. Unfortunately, he said, each time the demand went up, there were several practical men available—when, in fact, what was needed to deal with an impractical muddle was a theorist or a philosopher. Today, when trouble arises, the call goes up not for a practical man but for a theorist, a philosopher, or even, in some cases, for a theologian.

In my judgment, the fields of study and of intellectual pursuit which bear most

EUGENE J. MCCARTHY

directly upon politics today or which are of greatest concern to the politician are these: history, economics, and moral or ethical science.

Politicians throughout history have been, of course, somewhat concerned about their place in history and about the movement of history as it bore upon their own countries and their own political action. It has not been uncommon for great military and political leaders of the past to carry their own historians or, in some cases, to be the historians of their own achievements. They often ordered the construction of their own arches and temples and were the patrons of artists and poets who, in turn, were expected to do well by them in the artistic record. In the nineteenth and early twentieth centuries, the disposition to see one's own country apart from history, to assert its independence and unique character, was common among the Western nations. What passed for history or for political philosophy in too many cases was self-justifying and fictional. Extremes of nationalism are always something of a threat to historians as well as to history, since leaders of a strongly nationalistic state, or those who speak for it, are inclined to believe that it is somewhat above or outside history, and to think of themselves as the center and focal point of history, minimizing the efforts of the past and assuming that the patterns they established will be the model for the indefinite future. The questions of continuity and of relationships to the movement of history itself are discounted.

Nearly every politician today who says with some certainty that George Washington was the first president is said to have a sense of history. Such an observation in itself means little, but viewed in a broader context it reflects the deep concern for an understanding of history and a seeking by those responsible for government to interpret their own times and to make political decisions within the context and the movement of history. The search for historical order and context has been deepened and broadened in the period since the end of World War II. The history of the second half of the twentieth century cannot be written simply in terms of the growth and extension of Western civilization. All the continents, cultures, nations, and races of the world have become a part of contemporary history, demanding some explanation and certain inclusion. The simple doctrines of evolution, of economic determinism, of the culturally superior states as dominant, or the idea of history as projections of great leaders—none of these is adequate.

Carl Becker's words have come to be accepted as having particular pertinence today. "To regard," he said, "all things in their historical setting appears, indeed, to be an instructive procedure of the modern mind. . . . The modern climate of opinion is such that we cannot seemingly understand our world unless we regard it as a going concern. . . . Historical-mindedness is so much a preconception of modern thought that we can identify a particular thing only by pointing to the various things it successively was before it became that particularly thing which it will presently cease to be."

Not only are we influenced by the climate of opinion, but historical interpretation has also become of crucial importance in policy decisions.

The second intellectual discipline bearing upon politics in a direct way is that of economics. I do not mean to exclude other social sciences as having no bearing upon government and upon government decisions, nor would I discount the influence of science on our culture, but in a very special and direct way, economic theory has come to play a great role in government economic and fiscal policy.

Some attention was given to economics by government in the period of the Great Depression in the United States. Theories of business cycles were developed. What, in rather popular political terms, was described merely as Keynesian economics became the limited guide for political economy. Early in 1962, President Kennedy made the rather shocking suggestion that the President of the United States be given some discretionary power to adjust tax rates within limits and thereby make adjustments as to the amount of revenue the federal government would collect from the taxpayers. In 1963, the President asked not for discretionary authority to cut taxes but urged the Congress itself to cut taxes to stimulate economic growth and expansion. This was a new kind of argument for a tax cut. It challenged several accepted ideas in the field of political economy: the principal one being that in times of prosperity and a rising economy budgets should be balanced and federal deficits reduced; second, that federal deficits inevitably resulted in inflation; and third, that government expenditures by their very nature were wasteful and noneconomic. For one prepared to defend himself on these three points, it was almost as important to be prepared to make a moral case as it was to make an economic one. Economists and others, therefore, had to make it clear that they were not in any absolute or moral sense in favor of unbalanced budgets; not in any absolute or moral sense in favor of inflation—either galloping or creeping; that they did not believe that governmental expenditures were never wasteful. Each of these propositions, it was argued, had to be judged in the total context of the needs of the country and, therefore, related to the questions of war and peace and to the movement and condition of the economy, both domestic and international.

The second economic argument made against a tax cut and deficit financing was that such action would result in a larger deficit and, therefore, cause inflation. There were competent economists who argued that inflation would not result, but in any case, the prospect of inflation was held by some as sufficient reason for not taking the proposed action. This argument was based upon a mixture of economic and moral considerations. Speakers on the floor of the Senate asserted that whereas the greatest external threat to America was communism, the greatest internal threat was inflation.

Sumner Slichter, who has a reputation as a somewhat conservative economist, wrote a series of articles in 1959 dealing with the problem of inflation. In one of them, which appeared in the *New York Times Magazine* for March 8, 1959, he said: "There are ill-founded fears that creeping inflation will sooner or later become a gallop. Every country in Europe has had creeping inflation during the past ten years. The idea has become pretty well accepted that a continued drop in purchasing power of money is to be expected. And yet in virtually all countries the rise in prices between

1953 and 1957 was considerably less than in the period 1948 to 1953." He concluded: "Most important of all, people should realize that the alternative to creeping inflation is a fairly substantial amount of chronic unemployment. The problems of creeping inflation are a small price to pay for avoiding the much greater problems of unemployment and a rate of growth that falls far short of our potential."

The suggestion that expenditures or deficits might be used to move the economy from a relatively stable level of operation to a higher one was looked upon by some as an economic heresy. What the President and his advisers had suggested was that without a recession, at a time when the economy has leveled off at a relatively high point, it might be possible, through deficit financing—in this instance through tax cuts—to move the economy from that high level to a higher one without the intervention of a recession or of a serious falling-off in production. This approach was opposed by some; their opposition was similar to that which would be the case if in the field of physics we continued to insist that only the theories of Newton can be applied. This is to accept that we are condemned to a kind of closed economic cycle; it is to set our sights too low and to fail to appreciate our potential for economic growth and economic progress.

The third intellectual dicipline relevant to politics today is moral or ethical science. The influence of moralists is most often indirect. Strictly speaking, politics is not an ethical science or an extension of ethics. It is the function of morality to define the ends and purposes of political power and to judge the methods and conditions of the use of political power; but the combination and application is the work of politics.

Maritain has said that moralists are unhappy people; so are politicians. "When the moralists insist on the immutability of moral principles," Maritain wrote, "they are reproached for making morality relative. In both cases, however, they are only upholding the claims of reason to direct life. The task of ethics is a humble one but it is also magnanimous in carrying the mutable application of immutable moral principles even in the midst of the agonies of an unhappy world as far as there is in it a gleam of humanity."

The task of the politician is, in a sense, even more humble than that of the moralist. His is not the responsibility of making the decision but rather a more menial one of putting it into effect. The fundamental objective of politics is to bring about progressive change in keeping with the demands of social justice. Politics is concerned with ways and means and with prudential judgments as to what should be done, when it should be done, and in what measure as well as how it should be done. The politician, of course, must be a moralist himself, and he must pay attention to the voice of the moralist. It is most difficult to list any one man or even a few men whose moral judgments are clearly applied to political decisions.

The importance of moral principles is widely accepted today. There is recognition that principles about human dignity and freedom are the ultimate test of political decision. The concern of intellectuals in every field, and moralists, particularly, with the great questions of war and peace has had demonstrable consequences in the course of current history. The widespread interest in international organization and understanding and even enthusiastic support for the United Nations are more than a reaction to the savagery of the Nazis and Fascists and more than a reflection of the fear of war. The distrust of the nation-state and of excessive nationalism clearly reflected historical experience, but the movements supporting international agreement, international trade, and international understanding have a moral as well as a practical base.

In 1963, the Congress acted on two measures, each of which involved a very great moral commitment of the people of the country. One was the test ban treaty, the other the passage of the civil rights bill. The way for action on these was prepared to a large extent by men who had been discussing the right and wrong of the issues involved for many years: people like Reinhold Niebuhr, John Bennett, Will Herberg, John Courtney Murray, and many others, and pursued in such publications as *Commentary, Christianity and Crisis, Commonweal,* the *New Republic, America,* and others.

We have come to recognize that the mass of current history and the speed of history make special demands upon both governments and people in this last half of the twentieth century. The mass or the volume—I hesitate to say "of problems"—of those things which demand our attention is greater than it has ever been. Political responsibility today extends to the whole world. We can no longer set aside whole continents or whole nations or whole races as though they were not a part of contemporary history. We have to accept and, in some measure, give attention to all people in all places. There is no place in the world today and no person in the world for whom we do not have some degree of obligation and responsibility. This increase in volume is true in every area of human learning and of human effort—in science, in technology, in the structures of society. This quantitative change in itself would be a great challenge if we were to respond to it only as a static condition.

But along with this increase in volume, there is a second most significant consideration, and that is that the speed of the change and development and of movement today is at a rate which is faster than it has ever been before. We are called upon to respond not upon a timetable or a schedule of our own making—much as we would like to have it that way—but, rather, to respond on the basis of a schedule or timetable which the very movement of history itself imposes upon us. Man has more freedom than he has ever had before. He is more truly and completely human because he is more free from nature, more free from ignorance, more free from the material limitations of the past, more free of the past. On the other hand, there has been a growing separation between reason and life, between means and end, mind and matter, society and the individual, religion and morality, action and sensibility, language and thought, men in the community and men in the crowd.

I am not prepared to fix responsibility for conditions which do exist. Certainly, the changes that have taken place are not altogether the fault of theologians and historians and philosophers and men of letters. A limited case can be made for the treason of the clerks. In recent centuries, many—if not most—spiritual and intellectual and

EUGENE J. MCCARTHY

moral leaders, or those who have traditionally been so designated, were not as directly and immediately involved in the life and problems of their times as they should have been. They were guilty of indifference, detachment, and withdrawal. There was always the possibility that the gods could climb higher on Olympus and, by so doing, avoid the clamor of the world and of the crowd.

In the eighteenth and nineteenth centuries, there was a growing rejection of theology and philosophy, and even of history—an arrogant assertion that science and technology and new political and economic forms would provide the answer which philosophy and theology had failed to provide in the past. The excuse of rejection no longer stands. The world today is not arrogant; it has been brought low. The world today is not suffering from illusion; it has been disillusioned. There is, of course, still a need for the long view and for the search of absolutes, but there is a great need for the application of that knowledge which we do possess to contemporary life and problems. The dead hand of the past is less of a problem today—although we still use it as an excuse—than is the violent hand of the future which reaches back for us, imposing most serious demands.

There is little time to escape and few escape routes are still open. Some may wish to take the advice of Bob Hope, given in a commencement address a few years ago, when, in mock humor, he advised the graduates not to come out and face the world and reality, but to stay in. Or a similar escape taken by my nine-year-old son a few years ago. When asked what he would have preferred to be had he lived in Roman times—an emperor, a soldier, or a martyr—he declared that he would have preferred to be a lion.

Full withdrawal and retreat are no longer possible. Intellectual spokesmen and moral leaders are called upon today to prove the relevance of their ideas to life. By necessity of history rather than of choice, those who have long been pilgrims of the absolute have been forced now to become pilgrims of the relative as well. Intellectual and moral leaders today cannot retreat in ignorance and half-truth, or go back into their own protected caves. Leonardo da Vinci could speculate on the principles of aerodynamics without giving any thought to the possibility that his knowledge would be used to construct intercontinental ballistic missiles. Descartes could develop new theories of mathematics without anticipating that his conclusions might be incorporated in nuclear bombs. Men of the past did not have to anticipate what might happen to their ideas and their conceptions when subjected to the power of computers. Nor did they have to worry about chain reactions, as men do today, not just in physics but in biology, philosophy, theology, and in the structure and function of society. Time has caught up with the spiritual and intellectual leaders; their advance positions have been overcome.

The alternative to reasoned direction of life is a return to primitive conditions of ignorance and false fear. If one believes that man is the subject of history rather than simply the object, controlled by economics and by common will or by some other irrational force, if one acknowledges that the period of half-civilization and half-knowledge of the nineteenth century has been shattered, if one accepts that we must be prepared to face the judgment of our own person and of our nation and of our age, then the need is for a full and reasoned response. We must reaffirm our belief in the dignity of every person, our trust in humanity, and our confidence in reason as the one truly human instrument which we must use for guidance and direction as we continue to live on the edge of disaster.

Since man is a creature who, in the long run, as Allen Tate says, must believe in what to know and know in what to do, the intellectual and the politician both must continue to pass reasoned judgment on life and history, for without knowing, there can be no proper doing.

EUGENE J. MCCARTHY